HUCKLEBERRY HILL

*Child Life
in Old New England*

ELIZABETH GEMMING

Huckleberry Hill

Child Life
in Old New England

ILLUSTRATED

THOMAS Y. CROWELL COMPANY · NEW YORK

DESIGNED BY KLAUS GEMMING

Manufactured in the United States of America
L. C. Card 68–21602
1 2 3 4 5 6 7 8 9 10

FOR MARIANNE AND CHRISTINA

Contents

WINTER   *1*

SPRING   *55*

SUMMER   *81*

FALL   *111*

Suggested Further Reading   *141*

Index   *143*

Acknowledgments

THE four seasonal verses and the closing lines are taken from poems of John Greenleaf Whittier.

"A Melting Story" on page 25 and the tale of Memorus Wordwell on page 44 were adapted and abridged from *Introduction to the American Common-School Reader and Speaker* by William Russell and John Goldsbury. It was a typical and popular reader for intermediate pupils.

The old verse on page 85 is from a gravestone in the burying ground in the center at Temple, New Hampshire.

The lines quoted on page 88 are from "The September Gale" by Oliver Wendell Holmes.

The verse on page 97 is the third and last stanza of "The Fourth of July" by the Reverend John Pierpont of Boston, a poet and Unitarian minister and the grandfather of John Pierpont Morgan.

One of the young men who spent a week boating on the Concord and Merrimack Rivers in 1839 was Henry David Thoreau.

The small drawings of Indian corn (contents page), oats (page 109), and the dandelion puff ball (page 139) are from *The Grass*, published by G. Lane & C. B. Tippett for the Sunday-School Union of the Methodist Episcopal Church, New York, 1846.

The drawing "The Sugar Camp" on page 57 is from
John Gay; or, Work for Boys, Volume II, "Work for Spring,"
by Jacob Abbott, New York, Hurd and Houghton, 1864.

The wood engravings on the title page and on pages 40,
41, 67, and 82 are by Alexander Anderson (1775–1870) and
are taken from a rare book of over 800 proofs that is owned
by the Boston Athenaeum. Many were used to illustrate
religious tracts in the 1820's and 1830's.

The small cuts and ornaments beside the section headings
are from the Robinson-Pforzheimer Typographical Collection in the New York Public Library.

Uriah Smith, who drew the views of Temple (pages 60–
61) and Pepperell (page 134), was the author's great-grand-
uncle.

The author is most grateful to Catherine Fennelly of the
New Haven Colony Historical Society and Old Sturbridge
Village.

Special thanks also go to the author's husband, Klaus
Gemming. The idea for the book was originally his.

HUCKLEBERRY HILL

*Child Life
in Old New England*

"Winter Farm Scene" by George H. Durrie.
Private collection. Courtesy of Munson Gallery, Inc., New Haven.

WINTER

Blow high, blow low, not all its snow
Could quench our hearth-fire's ruddy glow.

IT was December in New England. The days were short
and the shadows long. The sun went down by four o'clock
in the northern valleys. The snowshoe rabbits and the weasels were safely dressed in winter white, and the muskrats
swam silently under the ice of the ponds. Hawks circled
slowly over the countryside. Weasels squeezed through stone
walls and along fences, stalking rats. Foxes barked in the
night. Owls hooted from the trees, and the moonlight made
the landscape silver.

By January a thicker blanket of snow absorbed the sounds
of people and animals and softened the shapes of the land.
The old familiar brush pile was just a mound, and the gate-
posts were old men in cloaks and cocked hats. The days were
like long twilights. The cows and sheep huddled together in
the barnyards, each one with a cloud of breath hovering
over its nose. Smoke rose from every chimney. Once in a
while sleighbells jingled.

There were two or three feet of ice on the ponds. The
men and older boys bundled up in layers of socks and com-

forters and went fishing at night, by the light of bonfires built right on the ice.

A freezing February rain coated every tree with crystal. The ice shattered like glass as it fell on the hard snow crust. The crust made walking a delight, but the animals of the woodland and the brave winter birds were frantic for lack of food. The wild grapevines were frozen cables, and every bud and berry was coated with ice. The chickadees came for the suet the children put out. Even the woodpeckers stopped to gorge on it.

 The homestead

Country boys and girls were expected to get up early and make themselves useful before school, to study hard, and to help out some more at home in the evening.

In winter the farm animals needed extra care. The drinking water froze in the troughs, and the snow drifted into the old barns. In the evening the farm boys littered the stalls, cut up potatoes for the sheep, raked down some hay for the cattle, and gave the whinnying horse his corn. Some mornings, the snowdrifts reached the window frames, and the boys merrily broke a path or even a tunnel to the barn, where the animals waited nervously.

Bringing in the firewood and building the fire every morning was boys' work. The fire was kept overnight by carefully raking up the embers and covering them with ashes. If the fire went out, a boy had to run to the neighbor's with a pair of tongs or a metal box and borrow a glowing live coal. (And if there were no neighbors, he had to strike a spark with flint and steel and catch the spark on charred shreds of

"The Younger Generation" by William Matthew Prior.
National Gallery of Art, Washington, D.C. Gift of Edgar William and Bernice Chrysler Garbisch.

linen. It took a long time in the bitter morning cold when the flint was dull and the tinder damp.)

First in the yawning fireplace came the shaggy, snowy backlog, perhaps a foot and a half in diameter and five feet long, drawn in on a hand sled and imbedded in the ashes. It was an art to select a backlog of just the right size, so that it would break in the middle and the ends would fall in just in time for raking up in the evening. Next came a forelog bolstered up on the "iron dogs," a middle stick, then a heap of kindling. On top of all came a pyramid of small pieces of wood carefully arranged.

By the time the rest of the family was up, a twelve-year-old boy could have a fine fire fizzling and spitting sap in the "keeping room," which was usually the kitchen. It was comfortable and warm there in spite of the drafts that blew through the crannies around the doors and windows. In winter, living without a fire was impossible, and it was a good day's work for a man or a boy simply to keep the fire fed.

Dishes, glazed stew pot, pie plate, and cup.
Old Sturbridge Village.

Country folk got up very, very early. Before dawn someone always went out to the barn with lantern and pails, to see to the animals. Once the cows were milked, everyone sat down to a bowl of bread and milk, or corn meal mush (or bean porridge) with salt pork, or some toast dipped in melted butter, or pie, or cheese.

At noontime people had their dinner: first, a boiled "Indian pudding" of corn meal, with butter or milk and molasses, and then some pork or beef with turnips or cabbage or parsnips or beets or carrots and maybe potatoes. Everything (even the pudding, sewed up in a bag) was cooked together in a big iron pot, and served heaped up on a pewter platter.

Supper was about the same as breakfast. There was a bowl of hot milk again with a tough brick-oven bread crust, or bean porridge again, or more corn meal "hasty pudding." Sometimes there were sausages, fresh fish fried in a long-

Treen: pitchers and a funnel.
Old Sturbridge Village.

handled iron "spider," hash, applesauce, baked beans with cider vinegar and molasses, or dried salt cod.

Plain farm families ate their heavy, greasy food from wooden plates called trenchers, or from pewter plates and bowls. They drank from wooden noggins or mugs of pewter or crockery. They seldom used napkins. They ate with their wide-bladed knives but they held their meat down with forks while they cut it.

After meals the girls scoured the pewter or woodenware with sand, and cleaned the cutlery by plunging it up and down in a pail of wet sand and chopped straw. Some fortunate households had water from a spring. The running water never froze. It ran into the house into a barrel, and the overflow ran out again through an outlet.

The forest pioneers used "treen" utensils—bowls and mugs made from trees. They often ate with wooden spoons from one large treen bowl for the whole family. They had little meat except for game. They enjoyed moose and bear steaks, and whole roasted raccoons and woodchucks.

"You must come over to supper at our house tonight! We are going to have the best supper you ever heard of!" cried one hungry New Hampshire boy to his best friend.

"What can it be?"

"Rye doughnuts, fried in lamprey-eel grease, with maple molasses—what do you say to that!"

Winter evenings

Many a farmer and his boys used their indoor hours to follow a trade, often in a small workshop or shed. Some made shoes and boots, or saddles and harnesses, or hats. Others made barrel staves and hoops, or earthenware pots and jugs. Part-time woodworkers made chairs, clock cases, tool handles, butter molds, ox yokes, furniture knobs, salt boxes, or wooden cups and bowls. Part-time wheelwrights made both wagon wheels and spinning wheels. Farmer-blacksmiths made nails and made or repaired pot hooks,

Iron traps and snowshoe frames.
Old Sturbridge Village.

trap parts, chains, rings for hitching posts, hinges, tools, wheel rims, sled runners and sleighbells, cowbells, and sheep bells.

Mothers took up their knitting and mending, or sewed their own red or blue or yellow checked homespun linen into shirts, towels, bedticks, bed hangings, and perhaps tablecloths and parlor curtains. They made simple gowns of linen or wool for themselves and their daughters, and broad, long aprons with gathered bibs, in blue mixed linen and wool for winter or checked gingham for summer. They

Wooden articles: piggin, bed wrench (used to tighten the
ropes that supported the mattress), funnel, covered bowl,
mortar and pestle, skimmer, and platter. *Old Sturbridge Village*.

altered the older girls' dresses several times to fit each littler
sister.

The children wore out their eyes doing their lessons by
the light of the snapping fire or of pitch-pine knots stuck between the hearthstones or by smoky, smelly oil lamps. Candles were hard to make and they were too much of a luxury
to use every day.

It was a special treat for a country boy to help his father
shell corn. They drew the dried golden ears across the han-

dle of an iron frying pan or shovel fastened over a wash tub, and talked about the Indians and the forests and the Revolution.

Children grew up knowing the value of everything in the household and the time it took to make it. They were taught never to waste anything. Girls did plenty of housework, knitting, and sewing, since everything the family needed was made at home. They even made their own cardboard stiffening for their summer sunbonnets by pasting layers of old newspaper together.

Many boys did odd jobs to earn a few pennies of their own. They saved up to buy a good jackknife, a country boy's most treasured possession.

Boys split pine shingles with their jackknives, and made maple shoe pegs to sell to shoemakers. Vermont and New Hampshire boys (and even some girls) made Indian brooms of yellow birch to sell or swap at the country store. They split the wood finely down to a one-inch core, shredded the split part, and turned it back and tied it. The core formed the handle. It took a boy three evenings to make a birch broom, and he usually got about six cents for it.

On winter evenings by the fireside, and on drizzly days in other seasons—in the garret amid festoons of dried apples

Hand-carved oxen and sledge. *Old Sturbridge Village.*

and peaches and pumpkin, or in a cozy corner of the barn, or beside a stone wall thatched over with grapevines—boys whittled toys for their little brothers and sisters and for their friends and, of course, for themselves. They made boats, oxen and carts, sliding willow whistles, windmills, water wheels, swords, and stiff wooden dolls. They whittled pop-guns from elderberry stems, hemlock bows and arrows, baskets from peach pits, and witch faces from hickory nuts.

They also made small household articles for their mothers—spoons and bowls, cheese-making utensils, butter paddles, and pie-crust edgers. They carved decoys, wooden parts for animal traps, and even fiddle parts. And they whittled spools and reels for the new cotton mills that operated on the village streams.

"The Tilton Family" by Joseph H. Davis.
Abby Aldrich Rockefeller Folk Art Collection, Williamsburg, Virginia.

Fathers liked to read aloud to their families. Newspapers were treasured, and never tossed out carelessly. *The Farmer's Almanac* urged men to use the long evenings well, and read for pleasure and instruction. The almanac hung in the chimney corner. It contained jokes, proverbs, puzzles, strange tales, home remedies, and household hints. It gave stagecoach timetables and the names of the tavernkeepers along the various routes. The almanac included a scientific farmers' calendar based on the positions of the moon, with planting and weather information and the times of sunrise and sunset throughout the year.

Every evening, farmers wrote up their day books and entered their accounts, often mixing the old English shillings-and-pence values with American dollars and cents. They seldom exchanged money, but they knew the exact values of every product and every stint of work, and they recorded all their debts and credits in terms of money values.

If one farmer helped another dig a well in the spring, and the second lent the first his horse to grind apples for cider that fall, they both kept a record. If they valued their services the same, they were "even." But it rarely worked out that way, and the books got very complicated. Once a year or so, the farmers tried to balance everything out and settle up.

Then Farmer Smith would take four bushels of rye directly to Farmer Holt to make up for the four bushels he had once borrowed from Farmer Keyes—because Farmer Keyes owed Farmer Holt something for salt *he* had borrowed the winter before. Farmer Smith also exchanged three bushels of turnips for a barrel of Farmer Frye's pork. The pork was worth much more than the turnips, so he agreed to pay off the rest of the "price," sooner or later, in cabbages and by the loan of his oxen to help pull tree stumps out of Farmer Frye's upper pasture.

Hopes and prayers

The people of New England were deeply religious and recognized God's place in their daily lives. The Bible was very often the only book a family owned, and they read in it every day without fail. Before the early bedtime came, each household gathered for family prayers. The father read a passage from the Bible and they all stood as he asked God's forgiveness and asked Him to watch over them during the long night ahead.

The bedrooms of the old farmhouses were unheated, and the sheets were icy cold. Several children often slept together in one bed. Children in the frontier settlements often wore the same thin shifts day and night. There were no carpets on the bedroom floors. The beds were heated with hot bricks wrapped in flannel, or with long-handled brass bedwarmers filled with hot coals. The bedwarmers had to be moved back and forth very fast or they scorched the sheets.

It was impossible to heat the drafty farmhouses evenly. Only the big kitchen was cozy. It was usually on the north side of the house under the long side of the roof, which slanted almost to the ground. In the great storms the clapboards and shingles loosened and the nails snapped in the frost. In the upstairs chambers, the children's bedsteads seemed to rock like ships in the whistling wind, and snowflakes sifted through the cracks in the unplastered walls.

Most people suffered greatly from head colds and fevers. Many weakened children died of measles and dysentery. Typhoid fever spread through polluted wells. Epidemics terrified everyone because no one knew about germs and contagion then.

Children's teeth decayed quickly and many boys and girls had painful gum boils. People simply rinsed their mouths after eating, or chewed twigs into rough toothbrushes. At every change in the weather, half the people had toothaches. Rotten teeth were often yanked out at home with a hammer and nail or a hook, for there were no professional dentists.

Sick people did not go to hospitals. They lay at home in a convenient warm room by the kitchen, called the "borning room" because babies were born there too.

The doctor

Most New England towns had a doctor, who farmed on the side like everyone else and accepted payment in labor or farm produce. Most country doctors had boarded in their youth with older doctors, running errands and caring for the horse and pounding drugs with a mortar and pestle until they had picked up enough medical knowledge to start out on their own.

Doctors set broken bones and bound up wounds and delivered babies. The only surgery they performed was amputation, and they tried to get that over with quickly because they had no anesthetics. The only good pain killer they had was a strong dose of powerful West India rum.

They were often as helpless as anyone else in case of a really serious illness, but they comforted patients even if they could not cure them. They made their house calls on horseback, with a candle in a tin lantern at night, and they brought their medicines with them. But most people trusted just as much to the old home remedies the earliest settlers had brought with them from England, and the strange herb remedies they had learned about from the Indians.

Accidents were very common in those days. Sleds and wagons crashed through bridge railings and overturned when horses slipped on icy patches of the road. Axles broke and wheels came off carts. People were knocked from their horses by heavy overhanging tree branches. Men were killed

"A New England Interior" by Charles Frederick Bosworth. *Massachusetts Historical Society.*

"Dr. Jesse Kittredge Smith," physician and surgeon,
by Ezra Woolson, age 21. *Old Sturbridge Village.*

in the forests by falling trees, and there were horrible accidents in the sawmills.

Children fell through the ice and drowned, and mothers and children fell into the open fireplaces. Boiling kettles spilled over, and dresses and aprons caught fire as housewives tended to the cooking pots that swung in and out of the fireplace on the iron crane. Lightning and chimney sparks set houses and barns on fire. Once in a while rats tipped over lighted candles in their eagerness to eat the tallow.

Most people just did not count on living very long, and they accepted sickness and death as acts of God. Yet in every village there were some people in their eighties and nineties who had been blessed with unusually strong constitutions and had survived all the fearful illnesses that took so many young lives. Most people felt that some pain and suffering taught children to be brave and considerate of the sufferings of others, but they dreaded the day when they might have to watch helplessly over a desperately ill child.

Worried parents tried one bitter remedy after another, or ten "cures" all at once. A strong child had to survive not only the illness but the added strain of all that dosing. If the medicines and loving care did not save the child, the family sorrowfully accepted God's will. The "passing bell" would toll from the meetinghouse belfry and soon the neighbors would assemble at the farmhouse to pay their silent respects.

 Breaking out the roads

There was plenty of snow every winter in New England, and after a blizzard the men and boys "broke out" the roads. There was no school, because no one could get through to the schoolhouse, or anywhere else for that matter.

Those who lived on the hilltops in the remotest corners of the district pulled on their knitted or furry caps and their shaggy blue and white mittens and their snowshoes, turned up their collars, and harnessed the oxen to their sleds. They often chained a log or a heavy board crosswise between the runners. Sometimes they used a big harrow weighted down by a pile of boys. The merry teams plowed through to the next farm, where they all passed the cider around and

Snowshoes, ice skates, and mittens. *Old Sturbridge Village.*

hitched another ox team to the sled. And they picked up another farmer and his sons.

Sometimes fifteen or twenty yoke of oxen, half buried in the drifts, strained downhill. The overworked teams, their nostrils white with frost, were dropped off to rest at somebody's barn. The boys threw snowballs at every girl's house on the way to the village. At every stop there were jokes and shouts and more cider, while the boys wrestled and rolled down the loose snow banks.

Teams and neighbors coming from other directions all met at the village center. Stamping their feet and blowing on their hands, the men crowded into the tavern for more refreshments by the roaring fire before they broke out the roads to the meeting house, the schoolhouse, and the doctor's house.

 The woodlot

People did all their heavy hauling in winter, over the smooth snow-packed roads and frozen rivers. For one thing, every man had to cut firewood from his woodlot and haul the logs out of the woods, ready to be cut at the sawmill in spring. The giant logs were chained onto sleds with runners or onto flat-bottomed sledges that polished up the snow for splendid sleighing.

The men and boys, many wearing shaggy mittens with leather thumbs and palms, went into the woods with the oxen or horses and sawed the fallen trees into sled lengths. They brought out the wood chips to save for fuel to boil the teakettle in the summertime. They saved the bark to shred and trade to the village tanner, who soaked it and used it to treat hides.

"Returning to the Farm" by George H. Durrie.
Courtesy of The New-York Historical Society, New York City.

Forest settlers even made boat oars from the tall pines right in the woods, and hauled the finished oars to the sea-coast on sleds.

The forest woodpiles, hovered over by snow fleas, were sometimes full of hidden treasures. Once in a while a tree contained a wild-bee hive full of honey, or a hoard of beech-nuts neatly peeled by the deer mice.

Tree after tree went down—knotty pine, maple, beech, oak, cherry, hickory. Their bark was scarred with squirrel scratches and the wider marks of raccoons' nails, and with holes drilled by woodpeckers, and worn initials carved years before.

Sleighbells rang out along with the ring of the axes. Every ox team or team of horses could be identified by the sound of its bells, for each set of bells had a different tone. The logging sleds carried big six-inch bells to warn other drivers along the narrow roads.

The men always saved a few of the wintergreen-flavored twigs of the black birch and took them home for the littlest children to chew.

Many towns paid their minister's salary partly in firewood. The townsfolk held chopping bees or wood haulings to make their yearly contribution of wood to the parsonage. Wood hauling was a holiday, and sometimes the women served the men a hot noon dinner of chowder, beans, and coffee right in the forest.

In other places it was the custom for the minister himself to serve a dinner to everyone who had taken part. At the parsonage the children helped twist strings to hang the roasts of beef and spareribs. Tables were set up in rows, and loaves of bread were neatly sliced and arranged.

The woodchoppers began to come in with great loads of straight fine wood. One came skimming down the hill, his horses' tails sweeping the snow, pulling the handsomest load of white ash cut that winter.

Two lines had been formed by the loads of wood thrown off the sleds to the right and left, almost the whole length of the parsonage yard. Another woodcutter sailed in from the farthest woodlot with the largest load of all. With speed and skill he emptied his sled in exactly the right spot, without any apparent strain. A moment later he had looked after his team, shaken the snow from his boots, and taken his seat at the table.

 *To market*

In winter many up-country farmers loaded their sleds with surplus farm products and made their annual trips to market to trade them for supplies they could not grow or make themselves. Some drove all night by moonlight to arrive at the market town by daybreak.

One Maine farmer arrived at Brunswick on a cold February day with a team of two horses pulling a sled loaded down with firkins of butter, bags and bags of dried beans, and three whole dead hogs.

Long processions of sleds from southern Vermont and New Hampshire used to line the roads, heading for Salem

"Inn Scene—Winter" (detail) by George H. Durrie.
Private collection. Courtesy of Munson Gallery, Inc., New Haven.

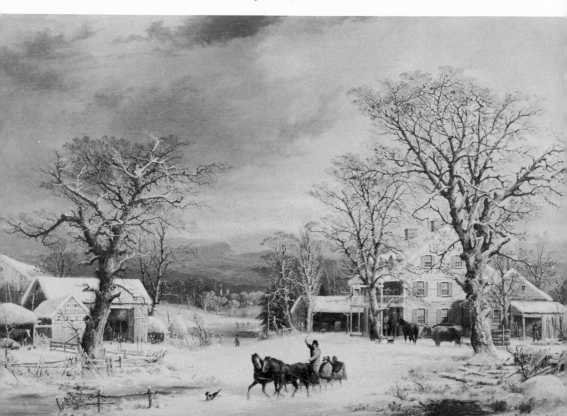

or Newburyport or Marblehead on the Massachusetts coast.
The homey taverns along the way were full of farmers having mugs of hot toddy in the clean-swept taprooms while the
old clocks ticked solemnly.

The New Hampshire farmers left home well before dawn,
for it was a five-day round trip to the coast for them. They
fed their oxen well and loaded their sleds with pork and
lard, grain, cheeses, beeswax, furs, and flaxseed, to barter
for a few bushels of salt, some tools or tinware or ironware,
crockery, a pound or two of tea or coffee, or gunpowder and
shot. They chose several yards of cotton cloth, some brown
sugar, dried salt codfish, a keg of West India molasses, and
a keg of Medford rum. If they had any credit left they
picked out a red bandanna handkerchief, some schoolbooks, or a string of beads and a couple of toys.

If the weather remained fair, the farmers reached home
again before dark on the fifth day. They took care of the
oxen, carried the lighter goods into the kitchen, and sat
down to supper.

 The country store

As the population of New England grew, and more and
more people settled far inland, they needed a place nearer
home to trade. There were not enough customers to support
a number of shops, so each town eventually had a general
store that carried "everything."

The stores carried rum and molasses and spices and dyes
and cane sugar from the West Indies. They carried printed
calico and lace, pins and needles and thread and buttons
and thimbles, crackers and cheese, salt and flour and tea,

flints and wire and nails, combs, paper, mirrors and glass-
ware, pewter and pots and pans.

They were a jumble of bins and boxes and casks and barrels. Everything was sold in bulk except for a few new patent
medicines that came already packaged. The stores were usually dark. The storekeepers claimed they had no room for
windows because they needed so much shelf space, and the
customers sometimes retorted that the storekeepers only
wanted to cover up the poor quality of their goods.

The stores carried colorful candies in dingy glass jars—
licorice, Chinese rock candy on strings, pink and white pep-
permints dropped in rows on sheets of paper. Salem "black
jacks" were dark and sticky and vaguely burnt-tasting.
Stone-hard "gibraltars" in peppermint or lemon or checker-
berry flavor came wrapped in soft white paper and were
quite expensive. (New England sea captains used to take
them on long voyages to eat when they felt homesick.)

The farmers came in to pick up the mail and the weekly
papers and read the auction notices and talk politics around
the stove or by the bench that always stood on the porch.
The storekeepers themselves had a lot of spare time to sit on
the bench and read, and many of them were shrewd and
witty.

Storekeepers liked cash, but they generally accepted
"country pay"—pork and beef, hides, tobacco, birch
brooms, butter, goose feathers, potatoes, flaxseed, apple butter, maple syrup, anything! They traded these country
products for credit at the big town markets where they went
a couple of times a year for their imported rum, molasses,
tea, coffee, and salt.

They also took payment in services and personal items:
knitted socks and mittens, homespun linen, woodchopping,

"Village Post Office" by Thomas Waterman Wood.
New York State Historical Association, Cooperstown, New York.

or vegetable picking. A farm wife might pay for her dishes, pins, and calico with a pair of shag mittens she had made, a basket of eggs, and the promise of her two husky sons for a few hours to help load the storekeeper's wagons. Many Massachusetts girls received credit or goods from the store by turning in work hats they braided from palm leaves shipped in bales to New England.

The storekeeper was a sort of banker, who gave credit

over a year or two and kept each customer's account, noting what he owed and what he still had coming to him. Hardly any money changed hands. The system was based on trust, and *an honest reputation* was a very useful thing to have.

"A Melting Story" (from an old reader)

One winter evening, a country storekeeper in the Green Mountain State of Vermont was about closing for the night. While standing in the snow outside, putting up his window shutters, he saw through the glass a worthless fellow grab a chunk of fresh butter from the shelf and conceal it in his hat.

"I say, Seth," said the storekeeper, coming in and stamping the snow off his shoes.

Seth had his hand upon the door, his hat upon his head, and the roll of new butter in his hat, and was anxious to make his exit as soon as possible.

"I say, Seth, sit down. I reckon, now, on such a tarnal night as this, a little something warm wouldn't hurt a fellow. Come and sit down."

Seth felt very uncertain. He had the butter, but the temptation of "something warm" sadly interfered with his resolution to go. It was soon settled, however. The rightful owner of the butter took Seth by the shoulder and planted him in a seat close to the stove, where he was so cornered in by barrels and boxes that while the country grocer sat before him, there was no possibility of his getting out.

"Seth, we'll have a little warm Santa Cruz rum," said the grocer as he opened the stove door and stuffed in as many sticks as the space would permit. "Without it, you'd freeze going home on such a night as this."

Seth already felt the butter settling down closer to his hair and jumped up, declaring he had to leave.

"Not till you have something warm, Seth. Sit down now."

"But I've got the cows to fodder and some wood to split and I *must* be a-goin'!"

But the grocer brought out two steaming glasses of hot rum toddy.

Poor Seth began to smoke as well as to melt! Streak after streak of the butter came pouring from under his hat, and his handkerchief was already soaked with the greasy overflow. Talking away as if nothing was the matter, the grocer kept stuffing wood into the stove, while Seth sat bolt upright, his back against the counter and his knees almost touching the red-hot stove before him.

"Confounded cold night, this is," said the grocer. "Why, Seth, you seem to perspire, as if you was warm! Why don't you take your hat off?"

"NO!" exclaimed poor Seth, clapping both hands upon his hat, "no! I must go, let me out, I ain't well, let me go!" A greasy cataract was now pouring down the poor fellow's face and neck and soaking into his clothes and trickling down his body into his very boots. He was in a perfect bath of oil.

"Well, good night, Seth," said the humorous Vermonter, "if you really will go," adding, as Seth got out into the road: "Neighbor, I reckon the fun I've had out of you is worth a ninepence, so I shan't charge you for that butter!"

 *Gay times*

Winter was the most sociable season, for it was easy to get around the district by sled or sleigh, and everyone had extra free time. The Sabbath ended at sunset on Sunday, so Sunday evening was a favorite time for get-togethers. It was a relaxed interval between the long, serious services in the meetinghouse and the chores of Monday morning. People were still dressed in their best clothes, and they made their social calls around the village. The big boys called on their sweethearts.

"Two Children with Dog Minny on a Pink Ribbon," attributed to William Matthew Prior. *Old Sturbridge Village.*

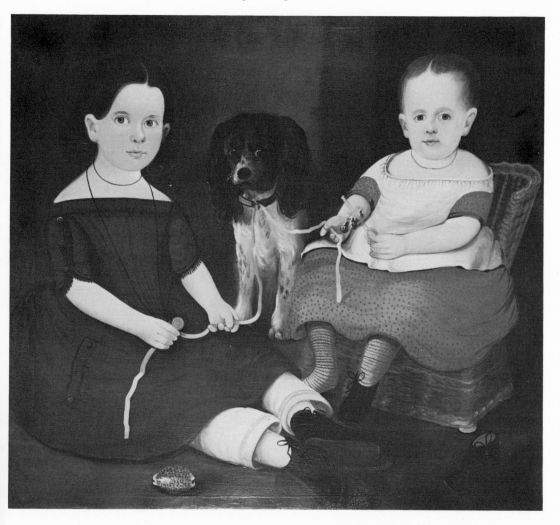

On fine winter days whole parties of neighbors and their children went on old-fashioned sleigh rides, often up and down the length of a frozen lake. The littlest children sat in wash tubs set on the sleds among bundles of straw. The merry travelers often put heated soapstones among the straw for warmth, and they bundled up in buffalo robes. Winter was absolutely the only season for pleasure drives; in spring the roads were thick with mud, and the rest of the year they were too dusty for comfort.

Country people were fond of late-afternoon supper parties. They came early and went home early. The women chatted and knitted in the front parlor, where samplers and

"The Quilting Party" by an unknown artist.
Abby Aldrich Rockefeller Folk Art Collection, Williamsburg, Virginia.

merit certificates from school hung on the walls, and family curios and treasures were proudly displayed. The men talked politics and town business in the sitting room.

Many a passerby, trudging past in the lonely darkness, was cheered by the glow from the windows of the snug homestead. He looked in and saw all the neighbors drinking tea from the housewife's best china (quite properly from the saucer, not the cup) and gathering around the table set with platters of cold meat, cheese, doughnuts, and apple pie.

Country weddings were generally held in the evening, by candlelight, with a supper for all the villagers. A wedding was a public event, and everyone was welcome.

Many times people gathered for "change-work" of some kind—they exchanged helping hands whenever one household had a special chore. All the neighbors came in to help, and eventually all helped one another in turn.

Quilting bees were fine excuses for a party. The women and girls worked several days at one house on one quilt, perhaps a fine wool flannel "pressed quilt" thinly filled with carded wool or cattail fluff, or, more likely, a patchwork quilt for everyday. The women shaped scraps of material into eight-sided pieces, and the little girls sewed the pieces carefully together to make the patchwork. The women backed up the patchwork with filling and lining and quilted the layers. Sometimes they quilted in squares or rectangles, and sometimes they used saucers as guides to quilt in rounds.

The quilt always seemed to be finished in the afternoon, and as soon as it was done, the men and boys came in for supper and a frolic.

In towns where people did not frown on dancing (as their Puritan ancestors had), the older boys and girls and the young couples went to balls at private houses or in the

The farther I fly,
The faster we tye.

LOVE

Valentine. *Old Sturbridge Village.*

tavern or the social hall above the general store. They danced the Portland Fancy and all the other old reels and country dances to the rollicking music of a fiddler.

In stricter villages where dancing parties were not allowed, kissing games, blindman's buff, and forfeits were popular.

Everyone, young and old, loved spelling bees. Young champions searched frantically through the Bible for long, showy words and names to memorize.

The young people went to singing school to practice hymns for the Sabbath services. The minister raised the tune with a pitch pipe or a tuning fork and they all worked on favorites like "Plymouth" and "Little Marlborough." Afterwards there was time for some old English and Scottish and Irish ballads. When singing school was over, they all walked home from the schoolhouse or the social hall, through the snowdrifts, by the light of the moon.

Most New England farmers lived far from the village center, in some "sightly location" with a view, near their farm fields and perhaps a mile or more from their nearest neighbors. When the great blizzards came, the families were completely cut off from the outside world.

Each household gathered in the keeping room to wait out the storm. There was food in the cellar and plenty of busy work to be done. They passed the time telling stories and rereading the almanac and the old newspapers and what few books and pamphlets they owned. Perhaps a week went by without the sight of a single soul from outside. They were snowbound.

"Baby in Red Chair" by an unknown artist. *Abby Aldrich Rockefeller Folk Art Collection, Williamsburg, Virginia.*

"The Sleigh Ride" by James Goodwyn Clonney.
Courtesy, Museum of Fine Arts, Boston. M. and M. Karolik Collection.

The red logs glowed in the fireplace while the north wind shook the old beams and roared down the chimney. The pewter gleamed in the open cupboard, and the family's frocks and cloaks huddled on their pegs in the corner. The old dog laid his head on his paws and dozed. A mug of cider simmered on the hearth beside a row of sputtering apples, and close by stood a basket of brown October nuts.

Country children were usually warmly enough dressed in wintertime, although most of them wore hand-me-downs and makeshift outer clothing. (Well-to-do children wore fashionable dresses and suits of imported cotton, and they

were not so comfortable!) Boys, like their fathers, wore wool-
en jackets and leather or corduroy or linsey-woolsey (linen
and wool) pants. Over these clothes they put on woolen
"long-shorts," smocks that pulled on over their heads and
came down halfway to their knees. Outdoors they wore
oiled boots or crude shoes shined with tallow to make them
waterproof. They wore knitted or fur caps.

The girls had thick shoes too in winter, and long woolen
gowns and aprons. Outdoors they wore old cloaks or plaid
shawls or blankets over their heads, instead of coats.

The countryside was made for coasting on homemade
sleds—boards with double runners—down hills terraced
with half-buried stone walls. Five or six big boys at one time
used to go sliding on large sleds on the roads. They paved
the inside of the covered bridges with snow before they
started out.

Boys wore out their homemade shoes sliding around on
the frozen mill ponds, and lured girls out on the ice and
tripped them up. They skated on clumsy skates, sometimes
nothing more than smooth bones strapped to their shoes.
During a warm spell the ice groaned and cracked, and the
boys raced out to do "benders."

The schoolboys of one New Hampshire town used to wres-
tle with an old buck sheep who belonged to the blacksmith
next door to the schoolhouse. The ram loved to have trials
of strength with the boys, and he usually won. One winter
day, when the boys had on hobnailed boots, they got the
sheep out on the ice on the pond nearby. The poor animal
could not get a footing and slid all over, and the boys threw
him down again and again.

Some days later, when the boys came by as usual and
dragged the sheep out on the ice, the sturdy old animal

threw them easily. The blacksmith, his master, had made him four little iron shoes with neatly sharpened cleats!

 The district school

Children made the most of the long walk to school, because it was a break between early morning chores and the awful prospect of six hours on hard benches. Knee-deep in snow, they pelted each other with snowballs. They burrowed in the drifts and dug caves by the wayside to surprise travelers. They ambushed passing sleds and swarmed all over them hitching rides.

The children played outside the schoolhouse until someone yelled, "The master's coming!" Then they raced in and took their seats, boys on one side and girls on the other, with a great clattering.

But on below-zero mornings no one stayed outdoors to play. One boy had the job of building the fire each morning, and if he came late or had trouble getting it going, the big boys blew on it and coaxed it along while the little children hopped around and wailed.

Most one-room district schoolhouses were miserable, much too small for the number of pupils of all ages who had to crowd inside. There were no playgrounds. The schoolhouses generally stood in the exact center of the districts, on some stony piece of town land that was worthless for any other purpose, far away from most of the farmhouses. They were often at a dusty crossroads on a poor triangle of earth, or wedged into the smallest possible corner of some farmer's field, with the schoolhouse itself serving as part of the fence. Sometimes a town had to set up large stones to keep passing

New England School" by Charles Frederick Bosworth.
Massachusetts Historical Society.

wagons and sleds from cutting the corner too close and smashing the schoolhouse.

A country schoolhouse was built to last. It was usually unpainted, "finished" with rough clapboards outside and plaster or nothing inside. The smoky open fire barely kept the temperature above freezing in winter, except right by the wide stone-and-mortar chimney that had been dug out like a honeycomb by hundreds of penknives. The children who sat up front complained bitterly of the heat, yet those in the back of the room were always cold and begged the master to let them come up and stand by the fire awhile.

The wind blew through the chinks in the walls and rattled the windows and blew down the children's necks. The corners were the coldest of all.

Even the drinking water froze in its bucket. After recess the boys and girls stood three deep in front of the fireplace, sucking snowballs. The curtainless windows were often broken, and the places where the panes were missing altogether were stuffed with wraps or covered with hats or pieces of paper.

Farm families often paid their school taxes in firewood, which the boys brought over on hand sleds and chopped up themselves. Children whose parents did not send their fair share of wood were usually assigned the coldest seats in the schoolhouse. Nobody ever seemed to think ahead and stock the woodpile with well-seasoned logs before the term began. The wood was always green and full of sap. Besides, it was usually soaking wet from the rain or the snow, because few schoolhouses had woodsheds.

The entry was mostly blocked by the huge chimney. There were pegs or nails for the children's jackets and cloaks and shawls, but most of the things ended up on the floor trampled in slush, and they were small comfort at recess.

Along the walls on three sides there were long backless wooden benches, shredded and worn, and full of carved initials. Sometimes a shelf nailed to the walls served as a desk for the older pupils, the "oaken benchers," who worked with their backs to the room. When they recited, they swung their legs over the benches and used the shelf as a backrest. The littlest children—the "a-b-c-darians"—were crammed together on wooden stools or slabs all the same height. The smallest children could not touch the floor with their toes.

The blackboards, if there were any, were simply smooth boards from the sawmill, painted black, but soon dull gray from use.

The older girls took turns sweeping the splintery slanting floor. The wind blew up through the cracks and knotholes

"Western view of Phillips Academy at Andover" by John Warner Barber. *Society for the Preservation of New England Antiquities.*

in the floorboards, and tough knots stuck out of the worn wood and tripped up the scholars. When a class was called forward to the center space, they "toed the crack"—a specific crack in the floor—to stay in a straight line.

A few of the big boys in their teens were patient and eager to learn. They struggled over their penmanship with the ten-year-olds. Some hoped to go on for a term or two at a nearby private academy or even to college. The future of a

bright country boy often depended on a sympathetic schoolmaster or minister who was willing to tutor him.

But most of the big boys were rough-mannered fellows of
eighteen or twenty who had never gotten around to going
to school before. They just meant to pick up enough learning to be able to keep their accounts and go through the
newspaper once in a while.

The district school was the only school most country boys
and girls ever attended. Some children showed up only on
days when they could be spared from the farm. Others did
not turn up at the beginning of the term because their winter clothes or oiled shoes were not ready in time. Still, nearly
everyone managed to learn to read and write eventually,
even if his grammar was bad and his spelling was peculiar.

☜☞ *The schoolmaster*

The winter term of school, generally taught by a man,
lasted as long as the town thought it could afford to pay a
schoolmaster. School terms were sometimes as short as ten
or twelve weeks. Most towns voted about ten dollars a
month for the master's salary, and often settled for the master who asked the least pay so they could afford a longer
term.

The schoolmaster was not a professional teacher. He was
sometimes just a boy from the town—perhaps even younger
than some of his rowdy pupils—who was trying to earn college tuition. Once in a while, "the master" turned out to be
a young woman. Sometimes the minister taught a term of
school.

Most likely, the master was a grouchy, even cruel, older

"Schoolroom: Teacher Striking Boy's Hand" by an unknown artist.
Abby Aldrich Rockefeller Folk Art Collection, Williamsburg, Virginia.

man who had no other way of making a living, but who had impressed the townsfolk because he could read all the big words in the Bible and wrote a decent hand. It was a rare schoolmaster who loved books and learning and also understood children and knew how to teach them well.

It was the custom in many places for the master to "board round," to live in turn with each family in the district during the term. In that way the towns did not have to allot money for the master's living expenses as well as for his pay.

Most of the farm families treated the schoolmaster to the best food they could afford, and sometimes opened the "fore room" in his honor. He sat in the best corner chair, book in hand, usually either feared or hated by the children of the house. In the evening the other farmers stopped by to converse with him respectfully.

If the master was patient and kind, he helped the children

with their lessons and even lent them his precious books of poetry by Shakespeare or Robert Burns. And if the master was young and lively, he entertained the family on snowy nights with merry tales of college pranks.

The big boys "declared war" on every new schoolmaster as a matter of course. In one town in the White Mountains of New Hampshire the boys showed the master they were in charge by throwing him out the window into a snowdrift.

"Barring out" was another old custom. When the master left at noon to go and eat his dinner, the big boys sent the little children home and barricaded the doors and windows of the schoolhouse from inside. They stayed in and clowned all afternoon, and the master was seldom able to do anything about it.

But one clever and athletic young master took a board, climbed the fence and up on to the roof of the schoolhouse,

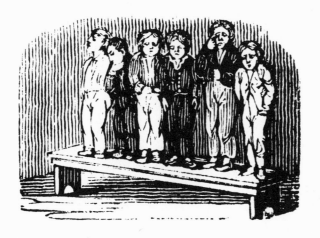

and covered the chimney with the board. It took only ten minutes for the smoked pupils to throw open the door and make peace.

 *The three R's*

Lessons consisted of endless drill and repetition of rules that were seldom explained by the master or understood by the pupils. They went on line by line, page by page, hour after hour. The master said, "Learn this!" with one eye on his birch rod, and most of the time the pupils did so, with an eye on the same terrible birch.

Not many children owned textbooks. Sometimes the only book in the room never left the master's hand. Most people could not afford to buy books, so country children used one or two scribbled, dog-eared old hand-me-down readers or arithmetics throughout their entire schooling. Children in the same class did not always work from the same textbook.

School usually began at nine with reading from the Bible by the oldest class. Then came writing practice.

The older pupils made their own copybooks from long sheets of rough brown paper folded and sewn down the middle, with covers of stiffer paper or wallpaper. They always wrote in ink, not pencil, and they had to mend and point their quill pens often with a penknife. The pens made horrible blots. The pupils ruled their copybooks with plummets made at home from melted lead hardened in a whittled wooden mold or in a straight crack in the floor. The ax-shaped plummets were tied with string to the rulers and carefully sharpened with a jackknife. Paper was very expensive, and in some northern schools the children used birch bark instead. They made their own ink from store-bought ink powder or swamp-maple bark, tea and iron, or vinegar and ox-gall. They often had to thaw it at the fire before they could start to work.

The master wrote a line at the top of the page for each scholar to copy. Beginners just got a row of straight lines. Later on they copied a row of curved "hooks and trammels," named for the black iron pot hooks at home in the kitchen fireplace. Advanced writers got a motto. Every child

"Horse in Full Gallop" by A. F. Davenport, a writing teacher.
Courtesy, Museum of Fine Arts, Boston. M. and M. Karolik Collection.

was expected to fill a whole page. Some masters handed out copy slips with proverbs and lessons.

Later, other classes read from the Bible, and the littlest children repeated a few sentences from the tiny old *New England Primer*. The primer was badly printed on poor paper, with tiny pictures and verses, the Lord's Prayer, and a catechism.

Quite a few children picked up the alphabet and learned to read at home with their mothers or their older brothers and sisters before they ever attended school. The Bible was their reader, and some of them had been straight through it from the beginning when they were only four or five years old.

There was a great deal of drill in spelling and abbreviations. The master gave the word from the "blue-backed speller"—Noah Webster's *American Spelling Book*—and the pupils loudly spelled out and pronounced each syllable in turn, and then the complete word, at the tops of their voices.

In their readers, the middle classes might have read the story of an extraordinary boy called Memorus Wordwell, who had learned the alphabet at home before he was two. He stood at the head of the class each year, even though his classmates were two years older than he.

At the closing exercises of his first winter term, everyone, even the minister, was amazed. "He can read in the hardest chapters of the Testament as fast ag'in as I can," said his mother. "I never did see nothin' beat it," said his father.

But Memorus Wordwell was a ninny. He did not know what the sounds he uttered *meant*. It never entered his head that words were written to be understood.

It happened one day that the "cut and split" for the fire ran short, and a boy called Jonas Patch was sent out to chop some wood during school time. He had been at work about half an hour when Memorus (who seemed to have less work to do than the others) was sent out to take Jonas's place "for a spell." He was about ten years old, four years younger than Jonas.

"Memorus, you may go out and spell Jonas," said the master. Memorus knew only one meaning for the word "spell," and he thought the master was granting him a chance at his favorite hobby. He was out at the woodpile as fast as another boy would rush out to play.

"Ye got yer spellin' lesson, Jonas?"

"Haven't looked at it yet. I mean to cut up this plaguy great log, spellin' or no spellin', before I go in. I'd just as soon keep warm here choppin' wood as freeze up there in that tarnal cold back seat."

"Well, the master sent me out here to hear you spell."

"Did he? Well, put the words out and I'll spell." Since Memorus was so distinguished a speller, Jonas did not doubt that he really was sent out on this errand. So our hero mounted to the top of the woodpile, just in front of Jonas.

"Spell *A-bom-i-na-tion*."

Jonas spelled: "*A-b-o-m bom a-bom*" (up went the axe) "*i a-bom-i*" (down it went "chuck" into the wood) "*n-a na a-bom-i-na*" (up it went again) "*t-i-o-n tion, a-bom-i-na-tion*"— and out flew a chip and hit Memorus on the nose. At that moment the schoolmaster appeared at the schoolhouse door.

"Jonas, why don't you come in? Didn't I send Memorus out to spell you?"

"Yes, sir, and he has been spelling me. How could I come in if he spelt me here?"

That was too much for the master. He wheeled back into the schoolroom, almost bursting with the most tumultuous laugh he ever tried to suppress. In a few minutes Jonas came in, followed by Memorus with his spelling book. Memorus exclaimed, "I have heard him spell clean through the whole lesson and he didn't spell hardly none of 'em right."

The master could hold it in no longer. There was one great roar from master and pupils. (The scholars laughed twice as loud because they were permitted to laugh in school time, and do it with the master besides!)

In arithmetic, most country scholars just about got

through division and a little work with fractions. They studied weights and measures for cloth, liquids, grain, land, and time. Three barleycorns made an inch, and the seven-penny nail, scarce but well known, was used as a measure of length for cloth. Two quarts made a pottle, and two pottles made a gallon. Two bushels made a strike, four bushels made a coom, eight bushels a quarter, and thirty-six bushels a chaldron.

The pupils learned "English" money and "Federal" money. "Old Pike"—Pike's *Arithmetic*—used English shillings and pence and was in use long after the Revolution. Children did their sums in English or American values or both, depending on the master. He gave the rule orally and they wrote it down in their sum books in ink, or on their slates with screeching slate pencils.

The children brought their lunches to school in baskets or pails. They had bread and butter or doughnuts or pie, and maybe a slice of salt pork or some dried sausages to grill at the fireplace. They pushed sharpened sticks through the sausage "links" until they looked like cattails, and roasted them for dinner, dripping grease all over their long leather or homespun aprons and the schoolhouse floor.

Then there were three more hours of school, with the same lessons as the morning.

Examination Day

From time to time the village ministers stopped by the schoolhouses to encourage the pupils and praise their progress. The climax of the term was Examination Day, when parents, the minister, and the town selectmen assembled for the closing ceremonies.

For weeks ahead, the children got ready for the day. They made handsome exhibition pieces of penmanship on loose sheets of paper to pass around the audience. They wrote in their best tiny script a sentence or two on Happiness or Education or The Art of Writing or Riches or Friendship or Spring, and made borders and flourishes and fancy initials to decorate the pieces.

They all practiced for the spelling bee, memorized poems to recite, and wrote patriotic compositions to read aloud. The very best pupils were awarded merit certificates written, decorated, and signed by the teacher.

Examination Day was a very serious occasion. More than one boy sat in restless misery, unable even to scratch his head, because his mother had combed sugar water through

Certificate of merit with floral border, by Rebecca Walker, a teacher. *Courtesy, Museum of Fine Arts, Boston. M. and M. Karolik Collection.*

his hair and it had dried slick and neat but stiff as a board.

The only good thing about Examination Day for most of the scholars was that it was the *last* day of school.

 Baking

The Sabbath lasted from sundown on Saturday to sundown on Sunday. Every Saturday morning the farm kitchens were a-bustle with the weekly baking, for no further cooking would be done until Monday.

The brick ovens next to the fireplaces had hinged doors and faced the kitchen. The oven was preheated until the fire roared, and when the fire had died down, the coals and ashes were raked out. The draught was closed and the oven doors were shut tightly. Soon the oven was tested. Then, with the help of the "peel," the long-handled oven shovel, the deep oven was filled with beehive-shaped loaves of "rye-and-Injun" and pies and the traditional pot of beans.

The tough loaves of rye and cornmeal bread were often overdone or underdone because it was so hard to control the temperature in the brick ovens. The bread baked three or four hours. Even the pies had tough crusts.

Doughnuts sizzled in a big kettle that hung from the swinging crane in the fireplace. Sometimes johnnycakes or shortcakes were quickly baked on a piece of maple wood in front of the fireplace.

Many New Englanders ate baked beans, with vinegar and brown bread, for Sabbath breakfast and also for dinner between the two services at the meeting house. In large towns the village baker used to come and pick up the bean pots on Saturday afternoon. He returned them on Sunday morning with a pan of brown bread to go with them. But in country homes the beans simply waited overnight in the oven for the Sabbath to begin.

To meeting

There was seldom any heat in the white wooden meeting-houses, and they were even colder for having been closed up all week long. The congregation huddled together through the long services, and the minister himself appeared in a heavy black cloak or greatcoat over his black suit, and with mittens and earmuffs. A few of the women brought small footstoves full of hot coals to keep their toes from freezing, but the men and boys did without.

"Church at Westfield Farms, Massachusetts" by George H. Durrie. *Museum of Fine Arts, Springfield, Mass.*

During the noon break, people who lived miles from the meetinghouse hurried to their friends' houses or the parsonage or the tavern. They warmed up with blankets, cleaned up the children, and ate their pocket lunches of cheese and doughnuts, beans, or pie, and refilled their footstoves.

The sacramental bread often froze solid unless it happened to be kept in a charcoal heater. Many parsons kept flasks of holy water under their cloaks to keep the water from freezing. No matter what the weather, babies were baptized soon after birth, and it sometimes happened that a poor January baby brought to the meetinghouse on its first Sabbath died from the cold and the long sleigh ride.

The typical old meetinghouse was a plain, lofty building. There was a raised altar and a pulpit with a trap door. The "slips," square pews with high walls, usually of unpainted, unpolished wood, were about six feet square. They had narrow benches around three sides, so that part of the congregation sat with their backs to the minister. Each slip had a door that led to the aisle.

The seats were hinged so they could be turned up when the people stood for the long prayers. The worshipers leaned back against the turned-up seats. At the "Amen" the seats went down with a banging that made the meetinghouse shake.

Tired toddlers put their heads down in their mothers' laps and took naps during meeting. Patient children were sometimes allowed to turn the pages of a small religious book, probably about some good and pious child whom God had already summoned to heaven. Weary little eyes studied bits of landscape framed in the high windows, or watched spiders spin webs in the corners of the slips.

One Massachusetts meetinghouse had twenty-four rows of high-walled slips surrounding the house upstairs and down. The walls all had railings around the top, supported by little hardwood balusters, fitted into round holes top and bottom. At the slightest touch they would squeak like nests of baby mice.

Bored youngsters stared at the round sounding board, like a turnip cut in two crosswise, that hung from the ceiling over the minister's head. With their eyes they measured the slender iron rod that held it up, and wondered how long it would take before the rod snapped.

Girls sat with their mothers in the slips. Indians and Negroes, if there were any in the village, sat in the loft. The boys often sat all together in the traditional "boy's pew" in the gallery. They behaved so badly that someone once called the boy's pews "Devil's play-houses." The boys scrambled up the uncarpeted stairs in their clumsy creaking shoes and wriggled in their seats like caged monkeys. In bitter weather they entertained themselves by pretending to toast their hands over the fiery red hair of some innocent fellow in the row in front.

At long last, late in the afternoon, people turned homeward, and when they arrived, each family gathered to recite texts from Scripture and discuss the two sermons of the day. The father read by the light of the fire from the huge leather-bound Bible and questioned the children on their catechism. The children read aloud from their primers or the Bible, and the father closed with a prayer.

The solemn Sabbath was at an end. Restless youngsters raced to get out their toys, and the grownups looked forward to a sociable supper party.

"The Reverend John Atwood and His Family"
by Henry F. Darby, age 16. *Courtesy, Museum of Fine Arts, Boston.
M. and M. Karolik Collection.*

H F DARBY, Painter.

"The Old Grist Mill" by George H. Durrie.
Courtesy, Wadsworth Atheneum, Hartford.

SPRING

The fox his hillside cell forsakes,
The muskrat leaves his nook,
The bluebird in the meadow brakes
Is singing with the brook.

B Y March the coarse snow was covered with weeds and twigs and the woods were littered with bark and broken branches and pine cones. One day there was a sudden thaw, and the south wind warmed the land. The roofs began to drip, and as they dried out they seemed to smoke in the sunshine. The trees in the woods made cracking noises. The snow softened, and little hidden rivers sprang up and made foamy yellow trails. There was a good drenching rain, then a freeze, and the snow took on a hard grainy crust that made walking easy.

 Sugaring

When the sap began to show at the ends of the twigs of the sugar maples, it was sugaring time. There was not much to do on the farm as yet, and every thrifty farmer with a few

"Canada Settlers in Sugar Camp in Snowstorm" by George Harvey.
Courtesy of The New-York Historical Society, New York City.

maple trees on his property made good use of them. The ten-pound loaves of white cane sugar from the West Indies were very expensive. Some farmers kept a hive of bees for honey, but many country people used no sweetening other than molasses and maple sugar.

The sap flowed best when the nights were freezing and the days were thawing. (Some people said it flowed best of all when the west wind was blowing, but stopped when the frogs began to chirp.) The maple was said to be a godly tree that did not run much sap on the Sabbath.

The oxen went right into the woods on the snow crust to drag in troughs or buckets, spouts, and provisions. In the early days men collected the sap in the Indian way, cutting a great gash in the tree and setting out ten-quart wooden troughs under the gashes to catch the sap. But gashing often killed the trees, so the farmers made notches instead, four or five feet up from the ground, and drove spouts into the notches. Some people collected the sap in troughs, others in tall narrow buckets of oak or pine with wooden hoops. The sap was stored in tubs.

The men cleared away the snow and built a fire and boiled the sap all night long in great kettles. The part that granulated was the soft sugar, and the part that would not granulate was the syrup.

Boys loved to go along to the woods and spend several days in the sugar camp. They tasted the sap and sugar and syrup at every stage, as they went along. Spring was in the air as the sap dripped from the spouts, and once in a while an early butterfly drowned in one of the sap buckets.

The sugar camp.

When the moon came up the older men told yarns around the campfire, tales of the Revolution, and tales of wolves and bears and wildcats. Icicles snapped, and owls hooted, and the boys moved closer to the fire to get out of the darkness all around.

If there were any houses near the sugar camp, the last afternoon was a merry sugaring-off frolic. All the girls arrived on sleds, and the boys and girls dropped the sweet new syrup on the snow to harden into chewy maple candy.

Mud time

One day, the farm boys' feet sank through the snow crust and their footprints turned into deep gray puddles. The crows showed up again to pick at last fall's brown and wrinkled apples and grapes. The woods were alive with woodpeckers and squirrels and blue jays. Everywhere, tiny paw prints crisscrossed the spongy snow. The pond ice groaned and shrank away from the shore, and the muskrats peeped out again. The minks began to look for mates to share their homes in the hollow trees.

The whole world was soon dripping wet. The cellars were soaked and the brooks roared with the spring freshets. The land was much wetter then than it is now, for the ancient forests and the thick matting of pine needles and moss and rotten wood, centuries old, held moisture like a sponge until the land was gradually cleared of trees and the sun evaporated the moisture from the open fields.

"The bottom of the roads fell out," and the mud—no telling how deep it went—held wagon wheels fast, up past the hub. People climbed precariously along the fence by the

"View of the central part of Princeton" by John Warner Barber.
Society for the Preservation of New England Antiquities.

muddy common. Covered bridges, built with roofs to protect the wooden beams and trusses, washed away whole, like boats, in the spring floods (and were later floated back upstream and attached to the banks again).

People just stayed home in mud time. (But to country children, mud time meant "six-weeks-to-bare-feet," when they could kick off their clumsy shoes for the whole warm season.)

While waiting for spring, the farmers and their boys built and mended fences to keep the animals from roaming at large and costing them a fine to get them out of the town pound again. The farmers also repaired tools, sorted seeds, and picked up the debris of winter.

 *Town meeting*

Town meeting usually took place in March as soon as the roads were passable. Public notice was posted by the selectmen, and all the voters (just the men, for women did not

"View of Temple, New Hampshire" by Uriah Smith, age 15.
Courtesy of Mr. and Mrs. Alexander H. Prinz.

vote then) assembled in the meetinghouse or perhaps in the
new town hall. The people of towns like Princeton and
Temple were shrewd and self-reliant, and they definitely
preferred to keep an eye on local matters themselves.

A prayer was offered to open the meeting, and town officers and a clerk were chosen to see to town business for the
coming year. All the voters discussed taxes, the schoolmas-

ter's small salary, the minister's pay and support of the parsonage, and the care of the few widows and orphans and town poor.

New Englanders tolerated anyone but a drunkard, and they treated a drunkard's innocent family with sympathy. In every village there were a few "queer" persons, mostly paupers and hermits, and the townsfolk usually grudgingly

FARES OF THE BRIDGE.

	d	s
EACH MAN AND HORSE		4
" FOOT PASSENGER		1
" HORSE OR MULE LED OR DRIVEN		3
" OX OR OTHER NEAT KINE LED OR DRIVEN		2
" SHEEP, SWINE OR GOAT		1
" CHAISE, CHAIR, SULKY OR GIG		8
" CART OR WAGON DRAWN BY ONE HORSE		6¼
" ONE HORSE BAROUCHE		8
" CURRICLE WITH TWO HORSES & DRIVER		
" WITH OR WITHOUT PASSENGERS		25
" FOUR WHEEL PLEASURE CARRIAGE		
" WITH TWO HORSES & DRIVER		
" WITH OR WITHOUT PASSENGERS		25
" FOUR WHEEL CARRIAGE WITH		
" FOUR OR MORE HORSES		25
" MAIL STAGE AND DRIVER		
" WITH OR WITHOUT PASSENGERS		25
" TWO HORSE PLEASURE SLEIGH & DRIVER		
" WITH OR WITHOUT PASSENGERS		16
" ONE HORSE PLEASURE SLEIGH & DRIVER		
" WITH OR WITOUT PASSENGERS		8
" SLED, SLEIGH, CART OR WAGON		
" DRAWN BY TWO BEASTS LOADED		
" OR EMPTY & DRIVER		12½
" EXTRA BEAST		3

Toll sign from Hartford bridge.
The Connecticut Historical Society.

voted a little money for their care unless the county had already established a "poor farm."

Town roads were high on the agenda at town meeting. Private companies had already built toll bridges and turnpikes, but the country folk often made long detours over the dangerous old hill roads, so full of rocks and stumps, because they wanted to avoid paying the tolls. Nobody wanted to spend town money either, but everyone had to admit that good new level roads through the valleys had to be constructed. Eventually most of the toll turnpikes were purchased by the towns or the states and kept up with public funds.

Wives and children waited at home for bulletins of the proceedings at town meeting, for there were often important issues at stake and some hot arguments. Little boys raced back and forth between home and town meeting, reporting the news. To the children town meeting day meant a pocketful of gingerbread when their fathers got home.

In the fields

After mud time the farmers plowed the earth and planted their crops. They planted the corn as the Indians had taught their ancestors—when the leaves of the white oak were as big as the ear of a mouse. Then they struggled with crows and chipmunks that stole the newly planted seeds.

They could not have managed the plowing and harrowing without their oxen. Oxen, each weighing fifteen hundred pounds or more, were ideal when strength was important but speed was not. They were not as nervous as horses, although they would act "hurt" all day if their driver snapped at them.

Oxen had to be shod at the blacksmith's. They got two-part shoes because their hoofs are cloven, like those of deer and goats. The oxen had to be supported in an uncomfortable sling while each foot was being shod because they could not bear their own weight for long on three slender legs.

"Summer Farm Scene" by George H. Durrie. *Shelburne Museum, Inc.*

The slow, steady oxen worked in pairs and wore yokes of elm or yellow birch. The farm boys rubbed the oxen's necks with linseed oil to keep the yokes from chafing them and making sores.

Boys began to help with the plowing when they were very young. Some four-year-olds even fussed and begged to hold the goad stick—not to touch the oxen with it—and just talk to them nicely. The following year, when the boys were five, they were able to drive the oxen all by themselves.

Older boys, around eight years old, "rode horse to plow." They rode the horse that walked ahead of the oxen as they tilled the crops. When the plow struck a stone, the whole team stopped short, and the boy up front pitched right over the horse's head into the soft earth.

There seemed to be endless hoeing and weeding and watering and more weeding. The little boys dug open the corn hills and killed the grubs and wireworms that lurked there.

 The village mill

In spring the sawmills began to saw into boards all the stacked logs that had been hauled out of the woods during the winter. By almost every good-sized stream there nestled a broad, low mill, which used water power for its operations. Some mills neatly combined their work, sawing wood in spring and grinding grain in the fall. The water was stored in one or more millponds behind wooden dams, and when it was let out all at once the rushing water turned the great old mill wheels.

Sawmills were very long buildings, twice as long as the logs they handled, because the saw was in the middle. The logs slid along wooden rails up to the coarse-toothed steel saw, and the water wheel that drove it was underneath. The trees from the virgin forests were terribly tall, and many of the pines were six feet wide at the base and two feet wide at the top.

Most millers made a good living because people always needed lumber to build houses and barns, and there were more and more people as the villages and settlements grew. The sawmill operators usually kept a certain portion of the lumber as their pay. Some of them also manufactured shingles, pegs, clapboards, tool handles, spools, knobs, wooden dippers, and measures.

One miller-farmer, who lived in New Hampshire, used to

pull on his short breeches and his knee-length blue-and-white frock and walk barefoot down the hill from his house to open the sluiceway at "No. 1 pond" to set the up-and-down saw going. The saw was pretty slow, so he went back up the hill again and milked the cows and ate his breakfast.

After breakfast he went back down the hill and rolled another log on the carriage, and crossed the road to open up the second mill pond. Around noon he went up to dinner. After dinner he opened the sluice on his third pond, and that kept the sawmill going until it was time for evening chores.

 *The meadows*

April seemed to arrive all at once with a rollicking chorus of songbirds in the still-bare trees—blackbirds and robins, phoebes and sparrows, meadowlarks and bluebirds. Hawks wheeled overhead watching the baby ducks on the pond. Father woodchuck emerged from his winter den to move his family of chattering babies to a new burrow in the clover. Dogs and small boys pestered him until he hid under the stone wall, but back he always came, bold and stubborn. The chipmunks woke up hungry and stuffed their cheeks with food. In the woods, the first struggling ferns pushed up through the tangled pine-needle carpet. Garter snakes slithered out of the rocks and walls, and frogs and turtles blinked in the warm sunshine.

Spring really burst forth in May, all pale green. The birds found their mates and built their nests. The swallows had come back as always, and the bobolink, the "skunk black-bird," was back in the meadow. The plows made rich brown paths through the fields, and the meadows were dotted with dandelions and violets, buttercups and daisies and clover.

Soon tiny wild strawberries would ripen in the golden sun, and after them the cherries, round and red and fat. The best cherries came from the sunny side of a garden tree, and in cherry time every tree would also bear two or three children wedged between the forked branches, eating and chattering with the birds. They especially loved the wild cherry trees that grew out of rock heaps here and there all matted with blackberry bushes and sumac.

Fishing

The fishing season opened with the first apple blossoms. The men and boys scooped up amazing catches almost everywhere. They caught eels and alewives in the rivers with scoop nets, and shad and salmon with huge seines that stretched across the entire width of the rivers. In the smaller streams they caught eels in wickerwork eel pots.

The Connecticut River was full of salmon then. It was also full of shad, and during the spring runs there were shad traffic-jams in the shoal water. The farmers simply gathered up the fish and carted them to their fields to use as fertilizer.

Shad were so common that some people were ashamed to be seen eating them. They felt that it was a sign of poverty because it showed that they had no pork.

Since hogs and cattle were slaughtered in late fall, and the best fishing was in the spring, New Hampshire people used to say: "We hope meat will last till fish comes, and fish last till meat comes."

Country boys listened to June bullfrogs to tell when the fish were biting. They tickled the bullfrogs' sides with sticks while steel-blue dragonflies the children called devil's darning needles zipped through the heavy air. Then, with homemade poles the boys pulled in strings of trout at "brooksmeet" or the "eddy hole," using only a bent pin and a worm. They caught shiners and suckers, pickerel and horned pout and yellow-bottomed "pumpkin seeds."

At night, the men went out to fish with nets and spears, by the light of pitch-pine torches or torches of birch bark rolled up tight and lighted.

Shearing

Sheep shearing took place after the lambs were born, in late May or early June, whenever the sheep could get along without their woolly coats. The best shearers were famous for their speed and their skill in removing the whole fleece in one piece, with hand shears.

Shearing was one of the festivals of the farmer's year. Like most big farm chores, it was turned into a community activity in many places, with neighbors helping neighbors until the job was done for all. The shearers competed with one another while the spectators cheered them on. One shear-

"The Latest News, Cattle in Stable" by A. F. Tait.
Courtesy of The New-York Historical Society, New York City.

ing, on Nantucket Island, lasted two days. Eight thousand sheep were washed in a large pond and then shorn by hundreds of men, while half a dozen tents sold refreshments to the crowd. That shearing was famous.

One Connecticut boy and his uncle simply took a gallon jug of cider and water for refreshments, and went down to the river outlet to wash their own sheep. The other village boys tagged along to drag the old ram into the water and duck him, and then wait for him to come out dripping wet and glare at them. The boy and his uncle built a railed pen

"Knitting for the Soldiers" by Eastman Johnson.
Courtesy of The New-York Historical Society, New York City.

and drove the wet sheep in, and a day or so later they
sheared them.

Sheared fleece had to be carefully cleaned of leaves and
burrs and tangles, and then carded, or combed, to fluff it up.
The fleece was usually pinned with thorns onto a sheet and
carried to a mill to be carded.

The mothers and grandmothers and aunts spun the
carded wool into yarn, once for knitting and twice for

weaving. They worked standing up, and as they stepped back and forth before the big wool wheel they walked miles. They did not waste the tangles that had come out in carding either, but spun them into coarser yarn. The wool wheel moaned mournfully, like the wind through the lonesome pine woods.

Both girls and boys were taught to knit as soon as they were old enough to hold the needles. Girls made their own stockings, and boys knit themselves suspenders and mufflers. Every family needed a tremendous supply of mittens and thick socks, and a nice pair of shag mittens was worth credit at the store, too.

 Muster Day

Muster Day, or Training Day, was the children's favorite holiday. They usually received a penny or two all their own, to spend on gingerbread.

All men over eighteen and up to their forties were required by law to meet several times a year for militia drill and practice, with musket, ammunition, and equipment. May or June training was the most important and festive in most places.

Early-19th-century coins.
The Chase Manhattan Bank Money Museum.

Before daybreak the farm wagons came from miles around and drew up close to the village green or the vacant lot where militia training was to be held. The horses were unhitched and tied nearby and given some hay. The biggest boys climbed trees for a better view. Booths and peddlers' carts stood thickly in an inner ring and sold hard Muster Day gingerbread, cider and root beer, rum and molasses, candy, and trinkets. The plain farmers ambled around with their checked homespun bandanna handkerchiefs full of the gingerbread.

At noon the soldiers dispersed for dinner, and the boldest of the boys peeked in the tavern windows to watch the officers eating. The girls lunched sitting on the grass or in the wagons.

The day ended with a thrilling sham battle, after contests between rival drummers whose drums sometimes measured twenty inches across and could be heard five miles away. When the guns were fired off, many a boy slid down from his tree perch as if he had been shot in the head, and sometimes the horses stampeded.

Few people really expected to have to take up arms and fight again as their fathers had in the Revolution. Many young men paid fines to get out of training. Respectable farmers disliked marching around with a lot of rough fellows who took the whole training exercise as a joke and turned the day into a drunken brawl.

A few officers took drilling seriously, but many company members showed up with rusty old dueling pistols, hunting guns, homemade clubs, and old patched drums. Some carried cornstalks instead of guns, and wore lilac boughs in place of plumes on their hats. They put their jackets on

"Militia Training" by James Goodwyn Clonney.
The Pennsylvania Academy of the Fine Arts.

backwards, and the thinnest men in the village borrowed
the baggiest pants they could find.

Those who took training seriously served in snappy vol-
unteer companies. The forty-eight members of a company
of "Grenadiers" organized in New Hampshire during the
War of 1812 wore handsome uniforms, sewn by talented
ladies of the town. They had coats of homespun blue trim-
med with yellow silk braid and bright buttons, and pants
and vests of white cotton. They wore gaiters of black velvet,
and black wool hats with brass front-pieces impressed with

the American eagle and plumes of white goose feathers with
red tops.

 *Traveling shows*

As the roads improved, more and more animal shows
toured the country areas. They always tried to come to a
village on training day or market day, when there would
already be a big crowd with extra pennies to spend.

For twelve and a half cents admission, a boy could see a
tiger or a camel, a buffalo, a pair of dancing dogs or a
trained pig, and a real monkey.

The wandering entertainers with freaks and dancing bears
gave their acts, passed the hat, and went on to the next
village. Traveling troupes of acrobats performed on small
canvas-covered platforms they set up on the green. A clown
arrived in town ahead of time and did a few somersaults on
the common just to be sure everyone knew the troupe was
on its way. That night, the tightrope dancer and the jug-
gler and the acrobats performed by the light of pitch-pine
torches, while farm wagons served as box seats.

 Over hill and dale

In the springtime, all the itinerant craftsmen and trades-
men set out again on their rounds and called at the lonely
farmhouses to offer their services and wares.

Cordwainers—shoemakers—went from house to house
to work up each family's tanned leather into crude, heavy
shoes that had no right or left foot. They set up their benches

and lapstones and awls right at the house, and they hand-
sewed the uppers and attached the soles with wooden pegs.
They also made fine cowhide boots, which would last a man
for life.

Traveling sign painters came through on horseback, carrying their stencils, brushes, dry colors, measures, and chalk
in boxes that fit over the saddle. The farm wives often hired
them to do colorful paintings, part freehand, part stenciled,
right on walls or panels, in imitation of the expensive imported wallpaper that was in fashion in the big towns and

"Interior of the Moses Morse Farmhouse, Loudon, New Hampshire"
by Joseph Warren Leavitt. *Collection of Nina Fletcher Little.*

cities. The painters were usually boarded at the house as long as they worked, and that was their pay. They mixed their flat unshaded colors—clay and brick dust and lamp-black—with fresh skim milk.

Painters often set up shop in the village for a few days, placed a notice in the newspaper, and accepted commissions for "face paintings," quick portraits on cardboard, complete with frame, for just a dollar or two. The only pictures that hung on the walls of most New England farmhouses in the days before the camera were portraits of the family, living and dead.

Weavers came to the door with their own looms and brought news and gossip. They sometimes let the children watch them as they wove, and gave them scraps of wool yarn for shoelaces and doll hair and hair ribbons. Most linens, however, were woven by hand at home by the women of the house—checked homespun bed-hangings, shirting, towels, aprons, sheets, pillowcases, spreads, and tablecloths.

Most housewives and their daughters made the family clothes themselves, without sewing machines or paper patterns. But sometimes the men's and boys' better clothes were made up for the coming season by an itinerant tailor who stopped by, spring and fall.

Skilled traveling chandlers brought their candle molds to the farmhouses and made up a supply of candles from the family's store of tallow.

Even nailmakers went from hill farm to hill farm and set up their own small anvils. They melted down scraps of iron from the farmer's old tools and cut them and hammered them into nails for him.

Yankee peddlers

The old-time Yankee peddlers set out as soon as the roads were dry, and traveled all spring, summer, and fall. Some of them were rough, suspicious characters with ragged clothes and dirty faces, shadowy men who suddenly appeared in the dooryard "out of nowhere" and terrified the children of the lonely settlements.

Sometimes college boys took to the road for a season to earn tuition money. Peddlers were generally famous for their humor and the gossip they picked up in their travels. They told good jokes and gave handy advice and compliments, and even did odd jobs like mending harnesses or making ink. They were always ready to make a new friend and another sale.

The peddler's wagon was jammed with goods: needles and pins and cards of buttons, shears, spoons and forks and knives, clocks, mousetraps, spools of thread, tin cups, one-dollar chairs, spinning wheels, combs and buckles, ribbons and lace, pots and pans boxed together with calico and gingham, spectacles, mops, ladders, and buckets.

The wagons had rows and rows of compartments. The peddlers sat up front, and sometimes rigged up large umbrellas in sockets for bad weather. In the rear, the baggage rack was usually heaped with rags and bags of goosefeathers a peddler had accepted in payment from housewives along his route. Brooms hung from the sides of the wagon and tin pails hung from hooks on top or underneath. The peddler made a cheerful clanking and banging as he drove up.

Peddlers usually carried English "penny toys"—wooden horses on wheels and painted jumping jacks on strings and whirling toy acrobats—as well as dolls, tin horns and jew's-harps, almanacs, and little chapbooks with woodcut pictures.

Most peddlers carried brightly painted Connecticut tinware. It was made from sheet tin cut out with heavy shears and joined together, and then painted freehand or stenciled. There were boxes for cookies and spices, plates, trays, graters, measuring cups, tea caddies, teapots and coffeepots, and pitchers. Tinware was very popular, for it was cheap,

"Yankee Peddler" by John Whetton Ehninger. *Collection of The Newark Museum.*

Decorated tinware of the early 19th century. *Old Sturbridge Village.*

shiny, and pretty, and much easier to handle than ironware. Peddlers also carried some miniature tinware pieces as playthings for little girls.

The Yankee peddler was a traveling novelty shop. He was a clever trader because he had to accept all kinds of farm produce and goods in payment and then sell them later on to someone else. Some fast-talking peddlers got rid of all their goods and by the end of the season sold horse and wagon besides.

Some people called peddlers "nutmeg men" because they sold whole nutmegs. Nutmeg was the most popular spice and it was expensive. A whole nutmeg always made a nice gift, and peddlers could easily carry lots of them and get a good price for them.

Rumors persisted that dishonest peddlers sold wooden nutmegs. One farmer was said to have purchased a whole pound of wooden cucumber seeds from a peddler—which only proves that if some peddlers were dishonest, some customers were stupid.

"Boys in a Pasture" by Winslow Homer.
Courtesy, Museum of Fine Arts, Boston. Charles Henry Hayden Fund.

SUMMER

For my taste the blackberry cone
Purpled over hedge and stone.

IT was hot and still in midsummer. The air was filled with
the scent of red and white clover and herd's-grass and
hay. The pastures were full of thistles. Cheerful little wild
canaries fluttered around the brooks. The black-eyed Su-
sans flourished in the glare of the sun, and yellow lilies
nodded along the sandy roadsides.

The murky woods were plagued with mosquitoes, and
small black flies attacked the workers outdoors. The streams
and ponds began to get low. Lily pads floated heavily on
the brownish pools. The muskrats had to climb up to their
doorways instead of diving down to them. The toad, welcome garden friend, appeared by the kitchen door every
evening.

 Summer days

The barefoot boys and girls lived every summer day
among the flowers and trees and weeds. They knew all
about the animals and insects and birds. They romped

through the fields and orchards, free at last of their heavy winter shoes and bulky woolens. The littlest boys wore loose playdresses exactly like their sisters'.

Children played many, many games, like tag and hide-and-seek and "I spy." Small boys waited eagerly as "jack-on-the-fence" by the village green, ready to chase balls in the meetinghouse yard and be rewarded with a turn at bat. Older boys also played rough, informal football with a ball filled with sawdust, or a pig's bladder covered with leather. Children swung on birch trees and played leapfrog and walked on stilts. Only the boys, not the girls, went swimming in the summertime, and they never wore suits.

For lack of store-bought toys, children made their own playthings. They made rag dolls, and balls from stocking ravelings and scraps of leather, and kites with dried golden-rod stems. They made pine-cone cows, and cornhusk dolls dressed in hollyhock skirts, and hobbyhorses from long crookneck squashes.

Country children knew all about plants—the velvety surface of a mullein leaf, the honey deep in the flowers, the feeling of wet grass between bare toes. Little girls lingered in the fragrant old-fashioned gardens, thick with marigolds, larkspur, clove pinks, sweet william, pink and purple asters, and dusty miller, and they wondered at the garden flowers run wild by the roadside, where the ghost of an old house seemed to take shape in the shadows.

"The Truant Gamblers" by William Sidney Mount.
Courtesy of The New-York Historical Society, New York City.

The early dandelion did as well as a buttercup to see if a
playmate liked butter. Girls split dandelion stems and put
them in the brook to make curls to hang over their ears, and
they made necklaces and bracelets out of them too. They
made earrings from the jewelweed and daisy chains from
the ox-eye daisy and the black-eyed Susan. They strung rose
hips into bead necklaces. They picked the orange "devil's-

paintbrush" to watch it close up tightly, and carefully took apart bleeding hearts.

Girls fed their dolls on "pumpkin pies" made of daisy centers, "cheeses" of the crumply seeds from the huge-flowered mallow, and "butter-and-eggs" flowers. They gave them milkweed milk in acorn cups. They dressed their dolls in clothes they made and dyed with bloodroot juice, and they sailed them around on leaf rafts in the brook. They swept up the crumbs under the Queen-Anne's-lace tables with pine-needle brooms.

Children matched blades of grass to see who would be "it," and they held blades of grass taut between their thumbs and blew through them to make them shriek. They sucked rose petals into their mouths with a pop, and blew balloons from leaves of the "live-forever" plant, carefully loosening but not tearing the underskin of the leaves.

The boys made ear-splitting willow whistles and slide trombones from pumpkin stalks and leaves. In the fall they made jack-o'-lanterns, and pipes and animals from horse chestnuts, acorns, and corncobs. They rolled themselves cigars from corn silk or wild grape stems, and smoked dried lily stems and sweet fern, the "small boy's tobacco."

The children snacked on pumpkin and sunflower seeds, sucked honey out of honeysuckle trumpets, and nibbled on grapevine tendrils. They gnawed on slippery elm bark, and chewed golden-brown hunks of spruce gum until it turned pink.

They captured grasshoppers in their cupped hands and waited for them to spit "molasses" or "tobacco." And they screamed at the dragonflies—the devil's darning needles that wanted to sew up their lips.

📖 *The burying grounds*

Children wandered in and out of the old burying grounds. They read the inscriptions on the old headstones, and wondered why some of them were clear and clean and others were encrusted with moss and lichens, as if God were trying to hide the names. They never, never stepped on the graves.

The earliest burying grounds were next to the oldest meetinghouses, built by the first settlers. They had turned into wild places, with tumbling walls and tangled bushes, far from most of the farmhouses.

People who lived in the hills wanted to bury their dead nearer home, and there were many small family graveyards, fenced in to keep out the cows, in the corners of the hay-fields or the stony pastures. There were large district "burying yards" by the roadsides, surrounded by granite post fences and iron gates, with rows and rows of tall thin gravestones of dark gray slate or light gray sandstone. The solemn unpolished stones were carved with weeping willows and sad round faces and cherubs with wings behind their heads.

> *Friend stand & behold as you pass by*
> *As you are now so once was I*
> *As I am now so you must be*
> *Prepare for death & follow me.*

The hand-lettered stone tablets were like ghosts, and it was terrifying to stumble upon one suddenly on the orchard path. When a farm was sold, its little private burying place was fenced in and exempted from the sale. There were many old graves by stone walls, but the walls tumbled with age, and the graves sank into hollows, overgrown with berry bushes and matted grass and yarrow.

 *Summer Sabbath*

The Sabbath seemed particularly quiet and holy in the summer. The cat sat in the corner with her eyes half closed, meditating. There was a special peace on Sunday morning. The villages hardly seemed to breathe, and people walked as if their creaking shoes were muffled. The birds put on a Sunday air and the cows did not seem to low from hill to hill as on other days.

"New England Homestead" by Samuel L. Gerry. *The Brooklyn Museum.*

The farmers sat by the kitchen window and gazed contentedly out over their fields. Only the most necessary work was ever done on the Sabbath: feeding the animals, milking the cows, setting the table, and clearing away (but not washing) the dishes.

Children were not supposed to play on the Sabbath except with special religious toys, like a wooden Noah's Ark with carved animals. Sometimes they looked at the solemn pictures in the heavy family Bible. Many children were punished for hair pulling and giggling and running races and berry picking.

The air everywhere seemed fresher, and everything looked much cleaner than on ordinary mornings. In fact, everything *was* cleaner. The houses had been swept and tidied up, and people had taken their Saturday baths and put on clean clothes. The older boys and men dressed in suits of broadcloth or homespun or in clean white linen frocks, instead of their usual homespun or corduroy breeches and smocks. The little boys often wore button-suits—a shirt-top that buttoned down the back and long loose pants that buttoned onto the top under the arms. The girls and women wore simple "best gowns," handmade at home of printed calico from the store, and straw or cloth bonnets. Most grown people owned only one best outfit, perhaps for life, and they kept it neat and clean.

Everyone took pride in "Sunday best." After sturdy work garments of scratchy, itchy material, even the boys felt more comfortable on the Sabbath. One seven-year-old watched, bitterly unhappy, in the great September hurricane of 1815, as the gale whipped the clothes from the clothesline. He never forgot his loss, and many years later he wrote a poem about it.

I saw the shirts and petticoats
  Go riding off like witches;
I lost, ah! bitterly I wept,—
  I lost my Sunday breeches!

They were my darlings and my pride,
  My boyhood's only riches,—
"Farewell, farewell," I faintly cried,—
  "My breeches! O my breeches!"

People came to meeting on foot, on horseback, and in heavy farm wagons. The village squire or the doctor drove up in style in a carriage. The walkers left home early, and

"Baby in Wicker Basket" by Joseph W. Stock.
Collection of Edgar William and Bernice Chrysler Garbisch.

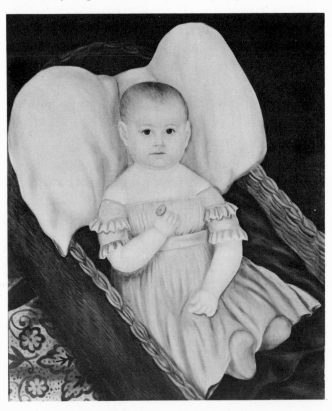

the riders followed not so very long afterwards. Children often rode in front of their fathers in the saddle. Many boys and girls walked to meeting barefoot, carrying their shoes in their hands and putting them on just before they entered the meetinghouse. (Most farmers and housewives and all the children went barefoot all the time in warm weather, except at meeting.) The big boys and girls cut across the meadows to keep off the dusty roads.

To pass the time before meeting, mothers and young children sometimes sat on milking stools or straight-backed chairs set out on the green by neighbors who lived in the village center. The men shook hands with one another, and their oldest sons hung around to stare at the pretty girls in their Sunday gowns.

At noontime the women and girls took their lunch baskets to houses nearby. The farmers lolled on the green and sweethearts strolled in the fields. Many of the children had a favorite spot in the meetinghouse yard, where serious-minded older girls told them Bible stories.

The heat of summer bothered people during the long services. Babies fussed and cried, and their mothers sat with them on the steps outside until they stopped. Many people, dead tired after a week of hard work in the fields or the kitchen, simply dozed off. One farmer's head would suddenly topple over to one side, while an occasional loud snort would show that someone had just awakened and was trying to make people think he was merely blowing his nose.

One day a certain minister could spot only one person in the meetinghouse who he was sure was really wide awake: his own son Samuel, sitting in the family pew beside the pulpit. The minister surveyed his nodding congregation and exclaimed in his loud strong voice, "*Samuel!* Wake up!"

Samuel's face was not the only shocked face in meeting that day.

Another Sunday, a lady brought her noon dinner of mince pie to meeting in a little cross-handled basket and put the basket under her seat. In the middle of the sermon a small dog sneaked into the meetinghouse, got under the lady's skirts, and began to eat up the pie. The lady gave him a kick, and with a yelp the dog emerged with the dinner basket around his neck. He backed across the pew and out into the aisle as fast as he could, and escaped with the lady's lunch.

One hot summer afternoon the gentle quack of ducks and the hissing of geese were floating through the open windows from the common. Two boys in the gallery had brought their fishing lines, which they baited with the leftovers from their lunch. They cast them out the gallery windows in front of the birds on the green. They got a bite, and for a few minutes the minister's voice was completely drowned out by the hysterical cackling from under the meetinghouse windows.

Once at home, children found it especially hard to pay attention at family prayers in the summer. Their minds wandered far and wide as the poplar leaves whispered outside. The late afternoon sunlight flickered on the whitewashed walls, and the sunset seemed to have set fire to the windows of a meetinghouse high on a hill in the distance. The children sat obediently and listened to their father, while they wistfully watched their pet kittens rolling happily in the yard outside.

"The Hobby Horse" by an unknown artist.
National Gallery of Art, Washington, D.C. Gift of
Edgar William and Bernice Chrysler Garbisch.

 School

The summer term of school was mostly for the girls and the younger boys who could be spared from the labors of the farm. Both the girls and the boys learned sewing. They hemmed brown linen towels and blue-checked aprons while the older girls made samplers to show their skill at stitching.

"The Country School"
by Winslow Homer.
*City Art Museum
of Saint Louis.*

The roasting sun beat down on the unshaded roof and the pine knots in the walls dripped with pitch. The littlest children dangled their legs from the benches and drooled and dozed. Bored little boys picked splinters from the hacked-up benches and strained to peek through the windows at the treetops and the sky, and envied the birds, who could fly wherever they pleased. The boys in their patched trousers

and linen shirts and the girls in their light dresses and sunbonnets longed more than ever for recess and the end of the
school day.

If the summer schoolmistress was young and pretty and
kind, the children brought her flowers from the meadows at
recess and decorated the miserable schoolroom.

The schoolhouse floor was wet with water from slate-washing and from the drinking pail. All the children scrambled for the same dipper. The oldest girls had the privilege of filling the pail at the nearest farmhouse well. The old well sweep, a long pole set in a forked stick, was heavy, for the handle end was weighted down with stones. It worked like a hand pump. A bucket dangled from the other end, and the stones helped raise the lowered bucket when it was full.

In some schools the children all ran to the well nearby to lower the moss-covered bucket themselves. They rested the bucket on the well and drank straight from the pail.

Sampler made by Fanny Bliss, age 12. *Old Sturbridge Village.*

"Snap the Whip" by Winslow Homer.
Collection of The Butler Institute of American Art.

At recess they played in the roads and fields and the forbidden orchards. The boys raced up and down the highroad shouting and hooting. They broke through the stone walls of granite and feldspar and pudding stones and went charging into the fields to turn somersaults. The older girls played games in the yard, while the little boys played marbles on the doorstep or messed around in the trash and chips of last winter's woodpile or sneaked around back to swap secret treasures.

The girls often followed the boys through the gaps in the walls to pick ferns and mint and romp through the mullein and thistles. Telltale paths crossed the meadows and led straight to the best berry patch or the wild cherry tree, where the children pulled off gum to chew. They brought armloads of ferns back to the schoolhouse and stuck them in all the cracks in the benches and desks and walls.

 *"Our Union"*

Most of the New England villagers were of English or Scotch-Irish descent. Perhaps there was a Frenchman from Canada, or a jaunty Irishman, or a family of free Negroes, or an Indian or two left from some ancient local tribe.

Each town had its "characters" too. Perhaps it was a pauper woman who lived in a shack and was said to be a witch. Or it was a rude, antisocial man who lived in a little stone house on a worthless tongue of land. The children from the schoolhouse spied on him, a stout fellow in coat and breeches glazed with grease and grime, an old Tory who prowled around his house and never left his place. Or the "character" was a beggar man who had served long before in the British Army and insisted on shouting "God save the King!" every Fourth of July.

Every town had its tellers of tales, old men who had served as fifers or drummer boys in the Revolution, some fifty or more years before. The village boys hung around the tavern stoop on Saturday afternoons and listened greedily to the old soldiers tell of Redcoats and General Washington, and the hills seemed to resound once more with the sound of cannon and smoke from the fires of "glorious action."

The "Spirit of '76" was very much alive in the young Republic, and there were grand celebrations on Independence Day.

Everyone went to meeting on the Fourth of July. The minister asked a blessing for "this universal Yankee nation," and there were patriotic speeches, poems, and hymns.

God of peace! whose spirit fills
All the echoes of our hills,
All the murmur of our rills,
　　Now the storm is o'er,
O let freemen be our sons,
And let future Washingtons
Rise, to lead their valiant ones
　　Till there's war no more!

"General Washington on Horse" by Mary Ann Willson. *Museum of Art, Rhode Island School of Design, Providence, R. I.*

The Declaration of Independence was read aloud at town festivities, followed by more short speeches and toasts —to "the Day," to the President, to "Our Union," to the "Soldier of '76," to the State of New Hampshire (or Vermont or Maine or Massachusetts or Connecticut or Rhode Island), to the Star-Spangled Banner.

There was a lot of noise from the firing off of some old fieldpiece and from the music of a military band. At noon there was often a public picnic, or a chicken dinner. The bells rang out all day long, and in the evening fireworks went up from the hills around town.

Raisings

Many men, especially in the newer settlements, built their own houses with their neighbors' help. Sometimes a master builder was on hand to direct the measuring, sawing, joining, and the actual raising of the building.

A house or barn raising was a great event, and everybody in the village went over to watch. The ladies chatted while the boys and girls raced around. The old men and boys whittled wooden pins to fasten the timbers, and the boys passed the pail of cider to all the workers.

When all the timbers were shaped and the holes bored and the joints made and numbered, the frame was laid out on the ground, wall by wall, and pinned together with the wooden "trunnels," or treenails. The strong men lined up shoulder to shoulder, with long poles that had pointed iron tips.

"Heave her up! Heave her up!" the master builder cried. They gradually raised one wall upright and held it until

another wall could be pushed up and fastened to the first.
Then came the roof ridgepole, weighing hundreds or even
thousands of pounds, and all the many beams and trusses.
Every joint was pinned with wooden pegs.

The host farmer supplied refreshments, of course, and
there was plenty of hard cider and rum. There were serious
injuries and even deaths if someone made a false step high
up on a beam or dropped a tool on an innocent spectator.

Town meetings voted money to furnish rum, sugar, lem-
ons, and cider for meetinghouse or town-hall raisings, and
were sometimes too generous. The entire meetinghouse
frame collapsed at one New Hampshire raising when a man
missed a joint. Several people were killed and over fifty

"Woodshed Interior" by an unknown artist.
Courtesy, Museum of Fine Arts, Boston. M. and M. Karolik Collection.

people were badly hurt. Not a single family in the town was spared at least some injuries on that day.

At a successful raising, of course, there was a noon feast and later gymnastics for the boys and young men—wrestling, jumping, running, and hopping races—to celebrate the achievement.

 Flax

Of all the farm chores, the most time-consuming was the production of flax, for making linen cloth. The whole family was involved, and the work was tedious and hard from start to finish. Almost every family had its cheery flax bed, gay with blue blossoms in early summer.

It was a real misfortune if the flax crop failed, or if something went wrong as it was processed and spun and woven. It took more than a year from flax seed to finished garment, but the cloth was tough as well as beautiful. Linen sheets and shirts and towels lasted through many generations (and many alterations to fit different members of the family).

In May, the children sowed the seed like grass seed. When the plants were three or four inches high, the children weeded the flax bed, walking barefoot among the tender shoots. Flax grew fast, and the plants were already ripe by the end of June or early July.

Then the men and the boys pulled the plants up by the roots. It was extremely hard work, hard enough to "break a boy's back" the first day. The plants were spread in the sun for a day or two and had to be turned several times so they would dry evenly. When the flax was dry, the men and boys "rippled" it in the field, dragging it through a heavy comb to break off the seed pods. Then they tied the stalks in bundles.

The flax then had to be "retted," or rotted, by being soaked in water for several days to soften and separate the fibers. After that it was put in the "flax-brake," which looked something like a stapling machine on legs, to part the useful fibers from the woody core. It was man's work, and so was swingling or scutching, when the flax was pounded on both sides to get out the bits of broken core and bark. It was slow and dusty work, and it had to be done in sunny, dry weather.

Little girls and older ladies often did the hetcheling, or combing, which was also dusty and tedious but easier. It had to be done several times, with finer and finer wire combs, to separate the long fibers from the "tow," the scratchy short and broken ones. Fortunately, many village mills took care of this step.

At last, the flax was ready to be spun by the mother or the grandmother of the family or by an aunt or a "spinster" neighbor. The long fine fibers were twisted into strong thread. Even the tow was spun into coarse yarn that would make a rough but useful cloth, commonly used for underwear or unlined shirts, pants, and shifts that were miserably scratchy any time and a real torture in hot weather.

Spinning was a skill to be proud of. Many girls dreamed of winning a spinning bee one day, when sixty or seventy small flax wheels were set up all at once and whirred through the day.

Whenever there was nothing else to do in a household, there was always spinning. Heaps of fluffy flax and tow were forever waiting in the garret. Farm women often took their babies under one arm and their flax wheels under the other and walked down the road to join a group of neighbors for a social afternoon of tea and spinning "until the cows come home." Then they hurried away again to milk the cows and set out supper for their families.

The pasture

The job of driving the cows to pasture in midsummer rotated from one child to another in many families. The pasture bars clattered nicely as they fell, and the stony pastures were full of delights morning and evening.

In early spring there were blue and white violets, and later on there was mint in the brook. The children picked their way across the boggy places, steppingstone by steppingstone. In summer the soggy soil dried out somewhat, but it was always soft near the millpond. On hot days the children poked with poles for water lilies while the cows stood knee-deep in the water for hours.

Around three or four the cows showed up at the gate with a clanking of cowbells. The boys drove them into the barn calling, "Coo boss, coo boss!" while the little children swung on the barnyard gate and waited for the supper call.

Except in winter, there was lots of fresh milk on every farm, but it soured very fast in hot weather. It kept better in the form of butter and cheese. Country housewives made their butter and cheese once or twice a week. June butter was the very best, because the new grass the cows were eating made a fine sweet-flavored milk. In early summer the housewives churned as much butter as they could and laid it down in round wooden barrels or firkins, covered with brine.

"Summer Landscape" by George H. Durrie.
Courtesy, Museum of Fine Arts, Boston. M. and M. Karolik Collection.

Most farmhouses had a special room for the churns and polished wooden bowls and milk pans and the clumsy cheese press. There were cupboards or shelves where the cheeses were set to ripen.

The housewife set out the milk for cheese in milk pans to scald in the sun. When the milk curdled, she broke up the tender white curd in a cheese basket and then pressed it to the bottom of the cheese hoops. Later the cheese had to be turned and salted and rubbed until the outside turned oily with age.

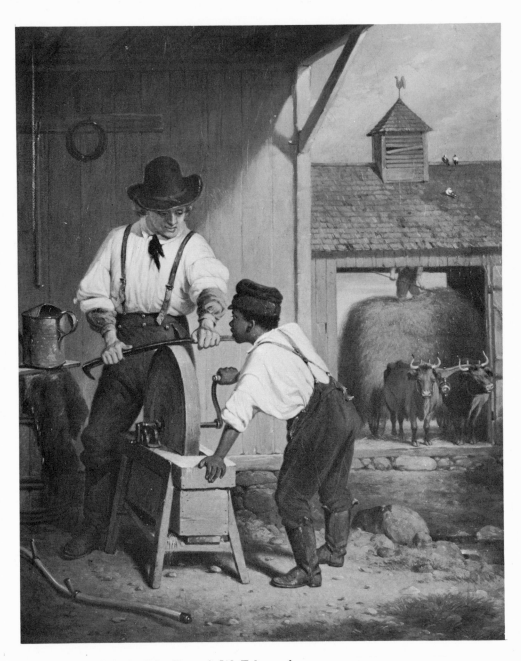

"The Scythe Grinder" by Francis W. Edmonds.
Courtesy of The New-York Historical Society, New York City.

New England housewives made plain cheeses and also crumbly herb cheeses, with tansy and sage, from treasured old family recipes.

 Haying

By the end of June the farmers brought out their grind-stones and sharpened their scythes, for it was almost haying time. Extra hands were always welcome then—day laborers, willing neighbors, even passing travelers who did not mind hiring out for a day or two.

The sweet smell of curing hay filled the atmosphere. At the nooning the workers went back to the farmhouse for dinner, summoned by the sound of a horn or a huge conch shell, or else they ate right in the fields while the oxen chewed on the clover and the horses munched the purple-blooming herd's-grass. Boys and girls ran about in the hot sun with lunch pails and jugs. The men grew drowsy in the simmering heat, listening to the bees droning and the grass-hoppers chirping and the millpond lapping nearby.

When the hay had been turned and dried, it had to be stowed away for winter. Some farmers used to say, "Two tons of hay for each creature in the barn." The boys learned to watch the sensitive oxen closely in hot weather. The oxen could not work well once they began to sweat, and the mo-ment one started lolling his tongue the boys got him into the shade right away before he "melted."

At the end of the day the hay, smelling even sweeter than it had when it had been new-mown, trailed from the carts as the oxen pulled them slowly homeward.

Bringing in the second crop of hay in August was sometimes wildly exciting. The afternoon sky turned angry and the clouds piled up—those yellowish cottony puffs that hay-makers dread. There was a warning rumble of thunder from over the mountain, and the farmers flew to help each other. The children ran around frantically while the patient oxen stared.

Suddenly the wind picked up and the hay began to blow about. Fat raindrops fell thicker and thicker until the storm finally broke. The rain streamed down and ruined the rest of the hay in a quarter of an hour. Then, just as suddenly, the amber sun shone again.

"Farmers Nooning" by William Sidney Mount. *Melville Collection at the Suffolk Museum & Carriage House, Stony Brook, L. I., New York.*

"West Rock" (detail) by George H. Durrie.
Collection of the New Haven Colony Historical Society.

 A breath of fall

Noisy August, with cries of locusts and crickets instead of caroling birds, meant shorter days and late-afternoon thunderstorms. The year was well past the turn. The flowers began to fade and the colors of the earth deepened. Red cardinals darted in and out of the trees, and yellow sunflowers and goldenrod dotted the land.

Hungry raccoons attacked the cornfields in the night, for the corn was full of sweet milk. The mink and her cubs went after minnows trapped in the low pools. The birds gobbled up the fat juicy grasshoppers that were doing so much damage to the crops, and the woodchucks just helped themselves to the beans and the leafy vegetables. Skunks dug their way under fences and stole eggs and ate the heads off some of the chickens.

Anxious farmers who met in their high-backed springless wagons on the dirt roads paused to talk about the state of their crops and their hay. They watched the sky for a while, shading their eyes with their hands, and worried about rain.

They watched their weathervanes more closely than ever. A shift in the wind gave them a clue to the coming weather, for they all knew from which direction came the gentle rains, or the sudden showers, or the dangerous squalls. "Cobwebs" on the dewy grass in the morning foretold a clear day. But if the cows were lying down, especially within sight of the pasture gate or the barn, rain was coming. The tree toads, shrilling through the summer afternoons, also foretold rain.

One year, as August passed into September, two young Massachusetts men set out in a boat to spend a week on the Concord and Merrimack rivers, heading up into the lonesome hill country of southeastern New Hampshire. They obtained their provisions from farmers along the way. The farm folk were hospitable and curious, for in those days a passerby from the world over the hill or around the river bend was a rare event. Strangers did not often walk the roads except to find work, and the young men were taken for umbrella menders because one of them carried an umbrella and for peddlers because they carried knapsacks.

Occasionally one of the young men ran along the shore while the other sailed the stream alone. They met again farther along. The one on shore told how a farmer had offered him a cool drink from his well, and the farmer's wife had given him a cup of milk, and the children had quarreled over the only transparent pane of glass in the window so they could catch a glimpse of the stranger at the well.

The two men rarely saw a village. There were woodlots and pastures, a field of corn or potatoes or hops or rye or oats or grass, a few straggling apple trees, and, at long intervals, a single house.

A small sandy-haired boy gazed longingly at their boat from the top of the river bank and asked his father if he might join them. They would have been glad to take him along, but he was still "his father's boy." The farmer gave them a loaf of homemade bread and some muskmelons and a watermelon. (He had a large melon patch and grew melons for the town market.) The young men left their tent and buffalo robes to dry in the farmer's corn barn.

When they returned to pick up their gear a few days later, the farmer and his wife and children were picking their hops. The same small sandy-haired boy sold them his very own watermelon "as is," still green, and the young men put it in their boat for ballast. They waved to the boy and headed back toward Concord as the first yellow leaves fluttered from the trees and fell into the still, smooth, melancholy river.

"Long Island Farmhouses" by William Sidney Mount.
*The Metropolitan Museum of Art, Gift of Louise F. Wickham
in memory of her father, William H. Wickham, 1928.*

FALL

Heap high the farmer's wintry hoard!
Heap high the golden corn!

SEPTEMBER days were still beautiful. The songbirds were gone, but herons and wood ducks haunted the marshes. Every berry bush was bright with fruit, and the air was full of thistledown. Sudden puffs of wind rustled in the treetops. The crows lingered, and when they alighted on a farm building, it foretold bad luck—a house struck by lightning or a barn not filled by winter.

"God's fools," mysterious wanderers, walked the countryside in the early fall. The farmers knew they had passed through, for they found their pumpkins and squashes marked with curious symbols cut with some unknown jackknife by moonlight.

Children gathered the "life-everlasting" and hung the gray-green plants with their clusters of round white blossoms upside down to dry out. Hedgehogs went after the sweet apples. Blue jays scolded in the trees, and red squirrels chuckled and dropped nutshells and clipped off ripe pears and apples just for the fun of it.

The boys and girls made friends with trees—the gnarled

apple trees, the ragged butternuts with shaggy branches and rotten cores that stood alone or in groups, and the lanes of fine old Lombardy poplars.

The fields were green, but the trees burst out in gorgeous color—the sumac deep red by the roadside, the scarlet swamp maple whose leaves children cherished as book-marks, the glossy purple beech, the yellow ash and birch and elm, and the deep brown oaks. Butternuts and hickory nuts littered the ground, and the children cracked them with their teeth or smashed them with a rock and gobbled them down. The pigs moved slowly over the earth gorging on acorns and beechnuts.

Red foxes watched the ducks and geese while chipmunks scurried about stocking their larders. The blue October sky was as clear and brittle as a windowpane.

Harvest home

There was no time to be lost in the fall, when great quantities of food had to be harvested and stored for the winter. The farmyards were strewn with casks and barrels, and loaded carts stood everywhere. There were pumpkins and cabbages, beets and carrots, parsnips and other root vegetables to be stored in the cellar, cool but protected from frost.

Pumpkins had to be cut up and strung on cords to dry for use in cooking and sweetening, and potatoes had to be dug. Fruit pies were baked for cold storage.

Grain had to be taken to the grist mill to be ground into meal and flower in case the mill wheel froze in solid later on. Boys of seven or eight used to ride three or four miles bareback to the mill with a two-bushel bag of rye slung over the old mare's shoulders. While the grist was grinding there was time to angle in the mill pond for a generous meal of fresh fish.

There was green corn to roast in the husks in the embers of the fireplace, and there were potatoes and whole pumpkins to roast too.

The housewives gathered herbs from the meadows and their gardens and washed them carefully and peeled off the leaves and petals to dry. They saved the stems and twigs and bundled them, and threw them into the fire sometimes for fragrance. They hung the herbs in the garret for use in cooking and preserving, for dyes and sachets, and to drive away mice and moths and flies. During the winter the herbs would also be used in medicines.

The country women used herbs like pennyroyal and joe-pye weed and tansy, lavender and mint, yarrow and

"New England Farm Landscape" by George H. Durrie.
Courtesy of The Connecticut Savings Bank.

Large jar by an unknown
Boston potter.
Old Sturbridge Village.

sage. Savory and marjoram, delicious in sausages, also relieved the pains of colicky babies. Mothers all knew how to
make tea from coltsfoot and flaxseed and honey to soothe
their children's coughs.

To store all their winter food the people needed tremendous amounts of pottery—jugs and jars and crocks and pie
plates, of redware or of hard gray leakproof stoneware,
decorated with blue painted designs.

 *Apple country*

In all the old orchards the children found tangy, spicy
apples—"pudding-sweets" and "long-noses" and "red
cheeks." They wore paths from their back doors to the walls

and directly to the best trees. The rule about orchards was that everyone had a right to as much fruit as he could eat or carry away in his pockets.

Apple trees die slowly and stop bearing fruit limb by limb. The old lone wild trees amid the currant bushes and the rhubarb seemed to have the prettiest blossoms in the village in spring, and their apples were small and bright yellow with brown-edged white spots. The last apples were the best of all. The upper branches of these trees were a tangle of forked sticks. Long poles lay on the ground below, abandoned by boys who had tried to knock apples from the overhanging branches. The bushes were always torn by children looking for windfalls or trying to hook fallen apples from the other side of the garden fence.

Ancient apple trees stood guard over the abandoned pasture burying grounds. But children never picked up windfalls from the graves. Only the happy cows reeled about, half drunk on the wormy rotten fruit.

Apple picking began late in the summer, and late varieties still came along well into the winter. The children stood on ladders until their arches ached, picking the pippins and poundsweets and Northern Spies. It was a tiring job and a serious one. Bruised apples and windfalls had to go straight to the cider heap. There were piles of apples in front of every house, and bins full beside the cider mills.

All hands had to help peel and cut apples into slices or quarters for slow drying. The pieces were strung on long homespun cords and hung in festoons over the chimney place.

More apples went into apple butter, and still others into rosy sweet October "apple sass" that would stand half-frozen in a wooden tub or barrel in the cellar or milk room all winter. The sour apples went on the bottom of the kettle because they took longer to cook, and the sweet ones went on top. Quinces were added for flavor, and molasses for sweetening, and the apple sauce stewed in cider.

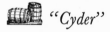 *"Cyder"*

Cider was everyone's daily drink, even the children's. It was cheap, and was freely offered to all wayfarers and tramps who chanced on a farmhouse. It was not apple juice, but hard cider, fermented and not too sweet. There was hardly a cellar anywhere without twelve or fifteen or even twenty barrels of cider for the winter. Whenever there was no fresh milk, the children drank the foamy cider diluted with water.

Country boys hung around the cider mills hoping for a chance to help out. The apples were enclosed in fresh straw in the cider press, and the press was turned by a horse who walked slowly in a circle, dragging the creaking sweep round and round. Wooden levers compressed the "cheese" until the juice gushed out in streams.

The crushed apples often clogged the holes in the press, and the horse was stopped while the boys scooped them out with sticks.

In cider time, the boys cut across back of the schoolhouse to pull up dried lily stalks or oat stalks from someone's field. They raced full tilt up the hill to the cider mill to suck the fresh sweet cider straight from the tubs. It was frothy as it squirted out of the press, and it was flavored with the juices of drowned bugs and caterpillars, and once in a while even an unfortunate bulge-eyed rat, soaking peacefully at the bottom of the tub.

"Cider Making" by William Sidney Mount.
The Metropolitan Museum of Art, Charles Allen Munn Bequest, 1966.

Golden corn

On fine October evenings some fifty or sixty merry people
—young farmers and their wives, and older boys and girls
(and some older people for dignity's sake)—gathered after
evening chores in a lofty barn for a husking. The golden
Indian corn was piled high in the middle of the barn floor.
Tin lanterns hung on pegs below the haymows, and the

gable windows high above winked in the darkness under the cobwebby beams.

Talking and joking and singing, the young people broke the ears from the stalks and husked them. They threw the ears into a pile and tossed the husks behind themselves. The children played hide-and-seek among the piles. When a young man husked a red ear of corn, he was allowed to kiss the girl of his choice. So most of the boys brought along a red ear or two in their pockets just in case, and some of the girls managed to sneak a red ear of their own into some handsome lad's hand.

The Farmer's Almanac disapproved of husking bees and advised sensible farmers to seat an older man between every two careless boys or they would have to husk the corn all over again.

The cornstalks were dried and stored for animal fodder, and the fragrant white husks were saved to make braided mats and stuff sweet, lumpy mattresses for the household. The golden ears were carried in baskets to the attic or the corn barn. The cobs would all go up to the garret later to be saved for light fuel.

Dried kernels would serve as "men" in the children's rainy-day games. And of course there would be some for fluffy popcorn, and sticky, jawbreaking popcorn balls, made with maple syrup or molasses and full of unpopped kernels.

When all the husking work was done, it was time for supper—baked beans, Indian pudding, pumpkin pie, cheese, doughnuts, apples, sweet cakes, and lots and lots of cider.

Daily bread

The farmers of New England grew their own grain—oats and rye and barley and buckwheat, as well as corn. Wheat did not grow well except in the Connecticut River valley.

The men used "grain cradles" to harvest the grain. The cradle was a combination scythe and wooden rack that caught the grain as it was cut. The cradle was very heavy, and hard to handle well.

The grain had to be threshed to separate it from the

"Corn Husking" by Eastman Johnson. *Everson Museum of Art, Syracuse, New York.*

straw. The farmers beat the sheaves with hand flails. They put the straw aside to use for animal bedding, and left the grain, hulls, and "beards" on the barn floor until the next dry, windy day. Then they opened both barn doors wide. They took the grain up into the loft and poured it down onto a sheet spread out below. The heavy kernels fell down while the wind blew the lighter chaff away (and also onto everyone nearby).

Every town had at least one grist mill in those days. The miller's children usually helped out in the busy season. The miller, like the sawmill owner, was paid "in kind," with part of the grain he ground.

There were two heavy revolving millstones, powered by the water from the stream. The miller poured the grain in through a hole in the upper millstone, and it came out at the edges, husks and meal mixed, and fell into a bin. The rye and wheat flours were "bolted," or sifted, through a cloth to separate the fine flour from the bran.

Cornmeal could not be ground so fine. Children usually took corn to the mill in small batches and brought it back unbolted, to be sifted at home. The coarsest cornmeal with the husks left in was fed to animals. The finest meal was for johnnycake, and the middle grade was for "rye-and-Injun."

 Winter clothes

Most farmers raised sheep, for meat and wool both. The old tradition was that New England sheep developed sharpened noses so they could nibble on the grass between all the stones that covered the land.

Many women wove their own woolen blankets and cloth, setting up their looms in a special weaving room or under the slanting roof in the kitchen. On warm summer days the thump of the looms echoed down the lanes as the village women sat at their weaving.

The fulling mills were especially busy in the fall, when the rough woolen cloth was brought in to be finished.

At the mill the cloth was washed in hot suds and scoured with "fuller's earth" and pounded and beaten with rollers or mallets to make it hard and smooth. It often shrank to half its former size. Then it was stretched to dry on tenter-hooks attached to the ceiling or sometimes dried in nearby meadows. Some fulling mills also dyed the cloth.

In every thrifty household in the fall, there was always a dye tub steeping in the warmth of the chimney corner. It was covered with a board and made a cozy seat on a cold evening. But there were often accidents with the dye tub, when someone overturned it and dumped hot blue dye all over the hearthside floor.

Blue was the favorite color and it was made from imported indigo bought from a peddler or the village store. In the cold season most of the men's and boys' "long-shorts" were of blue and white striped "frocking." Some wore jackets of "sheep's-gray," blue and white mixed wool, and nearly everyone wore heavy blue and white socks.

Work clothes were also colored with tree and flower dyes boiled in a kettle. Butternut and hickory bark and walnut hulls made brown, and peach leaves or mullein or oak bark made yellow. Dogwood made a kind of red, and goldenrod juice mixed with indigo made green. Sassafras bark gave an orange, and the juice of the iris a violet color. Imported madder made a beautiful rich red, and the purple wrapping paper that white loaf sugar came in made a deep royal shade.

"Going to the Cider Mill" (detail) by George H. Durrie.
Courtesy of Mrs. William Durrie Waldron.

Hunting

Fall was hunting season, and there would soon be fresh
meat to eat and a little extra income too.

People in the new settlements ate deer and moose meat,
and considered raccoon and squirrel a fine treat for breakfast. The wild turkeys of Colonial days were rarely seen, but
partridge, quail, ducks, and pigeons were plentiful.

Fur-bearing animals brought cash. One boy earned a

whole dollar, which was quite a sum for a boy then, by sell-ing the skins of two minks he had trapped himself.

The most exciting hunts were the passenger-pigeon hunts, in September and October. Then men and boys left on horseback before dawn. When they came to the right place they made ready their nets and stool pigeons, and lay down hidden in a bush hut, very still.

Suddenly there arose a deafening noise as a hundred splendid pigeons whirled overhead and settled on the ground on the net. A quick pull on a rope sprang the net, and fifty or more fine birds were trapped at one time.

In some villages the men and boys baited wild pigeons in a certain spot they called a "pigeon-bed," where the pigeons eventually learned to expect to find a feast. One day the men scattered the food as usual, but this time on a large piece of cloth. When the pigeons had settled, the men quickly folded up the cloth, trapping several dozen birds inside.

 Cattle

The cattle traders came through northern New England a couple of times a year. All work was laid aside, and school was dismissed if it was in session. Everyone rushed to watch the spectacle.

Many Massachusetts cattle, like summer boarders, were pastured in southern New Hampshire, especially on the slopes of Grand Monadnock. There were sometimes as many as a thousand head of cattle on the mountain, and the people of the region made their felt-like blankets out of cat-tle hair instead of wool.

The droves were collected again in the fall and passed through all the little towns and hamlets along the highway. Cattle traders, honest and not so honest, roamed the countryside. They knew every barn and pasture, and they hired fields on their route to pasture the cattle they had already bought.

The cattle drove approached a town with a rustle from far up the road. First there came a shuffling noise, then the sound of dogs barking and drovers shouting. The cattle kept on coming until they reached from the top of the hill all the way to the town line half a mile away. Dusty cowboys with birch switches kept the animals moving, but the drove seemed to have no beginning and no end.

At the end of the season, the annual cattle show gave many hard-working farmer boys their first sight of a real crowd, and their first visit to a large town, possibly the farthest point from their home and fields that they would ever see.

"Western view of Brighton (central part)" by John Warner Barber. *Society for the Preservation of New England Antiquities.*

The farmers drove their livestock to the center of the market town and milled around, self-conscious in their white linen holiday frocks. They were not at all used to standing idle on such a rare day off, when they did not even have to go to the meetinghouse.

The brisk wind of October had strewn the streets of the town with leaves of elms and buttonwoods, and the rustling of the leaves mingled with the lowing of the cattle. The wind continued to bustle across the countryside picking up loose straw. The farmer lads in their best trousers and flying corduroy jackets and fur caps went romping through the town, leaping fences and scooting along with the wind.

The old-time agricultural fairs displayed giant vegetables and stalwart animals, along with prize-winning quilts and braided rugs. All the boys and girls were dying to enter the sewing contests or the plowing matches.

The 1824 almanac gave a cheer for the fair:

> The great Bull of Farmer Lumpkins is a nosuch!
> Peter Nibble has raised a monstrous field of white beans!
> Jo Lucky's acre of corn has seven stout ears to the stalk!
> And, O, if you could only see 'Squire Trulliber's great boar! They say it is as big as a full grown rhinoceros!
> Huzza, huzza for the premiums! Here's to the girl that can best darn a stocking, and to the lad that shall raise the biggest pumpkin!

 Indian summer

For some days, the sun had come up gray. The vines were rusty and withered and the fields were full of stubble. The brooks were brimming full after the rains that had hammered on the shingles of the farmhouses in the night. The bare branches of the trees clashed together in the harsh wind.

But there were a few strange and beautiful days still to come, days bathed in the glow of Indian summer. The leaves were brown, but there was a rare wild feeling in the air. The corn shocks stood like tepees, and there was a golden haze over the hills, like the smoke from mysterious signal fires in the distance.

Or perhaps the season got its name because it was a tricky time, and it caught people off their guard. One day, in a whirling gust of wind, it vanished cruelly, and left the world grayer and more dismal than before.

☾ *Waiting for winter*

New England settled in for winter. The marshes oozed shiny mud and the water was dim and cold. It was quiet outdoors in November, with the pines murmuring and the dry seed pods and dead leaves scratching over the hard earth.

The muskrats finished their houses before the first frost. The sheep plucked scraps of grass among the withered mullein and panicked at every passerby.

The children's footsteps crunched over lightly frozen brown grass and rusty ferns. Things "showed" again, with all the leaves gone from the trees—large abandoned birds' nests and white rock ledges and faraway farmhouses and steeples.

The farmers checked and patched their barns and sheds and got ready to move the animals and the bees under shelter. They drove loose nails and fixed broken windows. They observed the animals of the woodland.

The wild animals seemed to sense the weather in some mysterious way, and the farmers trusted them. A bad winter lay ahead when the skunks left the woods early to move into winter quarters under the barn. It would be a long, hard winter indeed if the foxes sported heavy coats, and if the walnuts fell from the trees by the bushel, and if the muskrats built unusually large river-bank shelters. But if the muskrats built their thatched houses close to the channels of the streams, they were apparently expecting low water in the spring, after a mild winter without much snow.

Slaughtering

After the second frost, it was slaughtering time. Every farmer killed a fat hog or a fine stall-fed ox late in the fall. The weather had to be cold enough to chill the fresh meat and keep the hanging meat from spoiling. In some places, traveling butchers did the unpleasant job, but most farmers had to take care of slaughtering themselves.

Early in the morning they set a huge kettle of water on to boil over an outdoor fire. They lowered the dead hog into the hot water to be scalded and scraped. They carefully saved the bristles to trade in at the store or sell directly to brushmakers.

Most of the meat was "put down" for winter. But for a change there would be some fresh meat—spareribs to be shared with the neighbors, who would share theirs a few days later when they did their slaughtering.

Corn-fed pork had a fine, rich flavor fresh, salted, or

smoked. There were lots of fresh sausages, and many more sausages to be dried and hung for storage. Huge amounts of pork were salted in crocks or barrels and put down in the cellar. Hams and shoulders were "corned" in brine or smoked in the chimney, in sweet thick smoke from a fire of chopped dried corncobs.

The farmers' wives salted down a barrel of beef in the early winter too. They hung the beef "hams," lightly salted, in the chimney a few days to dry out, for "hung beef" was as important as bread.

 Soap

Country people made their own soap. They had carefully saved wood ashes from the fireplace in a barrel with layers of straw, and they slowly poured water over the ashes to make lye, which trickled out into a bucket. The lye had to be very strong.

There were pounds and pounds of animal fat from slaughtering, and the housewives had also carefully saved every bit of waste grease from cooking.

The men and boys boiled the lye and the grease together in a great iron kettle outdoors. They had to stir the awful-smelling mixture constantly, and it did not always turn out well even so.

The soap was soft and jellylike, but it was extremely strong and harsh. It was used mainly for the family wash, and nobody liked to use it on his own skin.

Some families caught rain water in a barrel to use on washday, and others used well water. In the winter, when the well was frozen over, one of the boys sometimes had to go to the river or pond, break the ice, and haul tubs of water back home by ox sled.

Every Monday, the steaming tubs of hot water waited on the porch or in the kitchen for the weekly laundry. The tubs were often dragged to the well for the final rinse. The women kept looking anxiously at the sky for signs of rain. After the white wash was hung out on the line, the children had to look out for the old horse and see that he did not walk under the flapping sheets and shirts and get them dirty all over again.

 Thanksgiving

The crowning feast of the farmer's year was Thanksgiving, when everyone gathered together from far and near to give thanks for ruddy apples and golden grain, for all the gifts of field and orchard.

Since all the people raised and produced everything they needed to live on, from food to clothing, Thanksgiving was a serious and truly meaningful holiday. All the family, perhaps for just that one day a year, traveled "home" to be together—relatives who had moved away, boys apprenticed to a craftsman in the city, cousins seen but once a year.

The Puritans had left their English homes and come to Massachusetts in the seventeenth century in protest against what they called the worldly and frivolous customs of the English Church. They meant to purify their religion, and worship plainly as of old. Merry Christmas celebrations were too much a part of what they had rejected when they

"Home to Thanksgiving" by Currier and Ives, after a painting by George H. Durrie. *The Harry T. Peters Collection, Museum of the City of New York.*

sailed away to the New World, and their serious, thoughtful New England descendants had not yet gotten over their suspicions of Christmas festivities.

In spirit, Thanksgiving was a religious holiday. Ten days ahead of time the minister read the Governor's Proclamation in meeting, noting both "the year of our Lord" and "the year of the independence of the United States of America." On the Sabbath before Thanksgiving Day, a collection was taken up for the poor, and the children begged their mothers for a coin to give.

On Thanksgiving morning, everyone went to meeting.

Then came the feast. The big Thanksgiving turkeys were roasted on a spit over the open fire. In some homes, they were roasted in a "tin kitchen," a sort of reflecting oven set in the fireplace. For once, the children did not mind scorching their faces as they turned the spit in honor of the annual festival.

The traditional pumpkin pie was made with molasses. Occasionally a town even postponed its Thanksgiving observance because there was no molasses to be had. Then, when a barrel could be brought in some days later, they had their feast.

Well-to-do families enjoyed very grand Thanksgiving dinners. Dinner lasted two whole hours, and there were twenty or thirty relatives present. The boys and girls sat at a special side table, and the oldest cousins told such funny stories about school that the children roared with laughter.

Dinner began with chicken pies, and then came the roasted turkey. The diners all ate as much as they could before starting in on the pies, mince and squash and lemony Marlborough, and the cranberry tarts and the plum pud-

Toy horse. *Old Sturbridge Village.*　　　　Toy cow. *Old Sturbridge Village.*

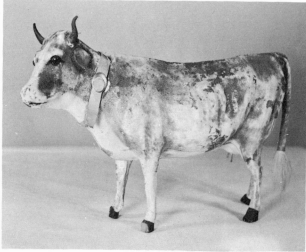

ding. For dessert there were also dried fruits—dates and raisins and figs—and lots of nuts. The children broke open the walnuts carefully and took out the "roast turkey" shapes inside.

After dinner the children played Old Maid, and as the afternoon wore on, there was only one proper game for boys. That game was football.

The forest settlers of the north especially liked to make Thanksgiving last for two days. It was the custom in the hill country for several families to dine together at one homestead on the first day and at another homestead on the second.

The women cooked a sample of each food raised during the year past, and placed it on the table as a symbol of their gratitude. There was a longer grace than usual. As always, the people stood around the table as the head of the house asked a blessing, and they stood again at the end of the meal when he "returned thanks." For dinner there was a round Indian pudding and a "boiled dish" of pork or mutton with a variety of vegetables, baked meats and fowls, pies, and cider.

 Taking leave

For more and more New England families, however, October's golden harvest days were losing much of their old meaning. Many farmers began to realize that for New England, farming was not the way of the future.

The hill farms were bleak and lonely, and the granite soil had quickly washed away. After the rich leaf mold of centuries was worn out, the crops were disappointing.

"Joseph and Anna Raymond" by an unknown artist.
The Metropolitan Museum of Art, Gift of Edgar William and Bernice Chrysler Garbisch, 1966.

"View of Babbatassett Village, Pepperell, Massachusetts" (detail) by Uriah Smith, age 19. *Courtesy of Mr. and Mrs. Paul Bonynge, Jr.*

There were several "poverty years" of unseasonable cold. In the famous cold year of 1816 it snowed even in July and August, and there was a frost in every month of the year. There were almost no crops at all, and some people had to live on oatmeal, boiled thistles, fried weeds, wild turnips, and hedgehogs. There was hardly enough corn for the next year's seeds. A June blizzard killed all the new plants, and the newly sheared sheep died of the cold.

Many discouraged farmers abandoned their small homesteads and headed south or west, to New York and Pennsylvania and Ohio and Indiana and Illinois. There, they found magnificent level farmland, well suited to raising wheat and corn and livestock. The flat land was easy to cultivate on a large scale, with farm machinery, and the brand-new Erie Canal and the fast-growing railroads were ready to carry the excellent western flour and meat back east for sale.

Many districts of New England were dotted with cellar

holes overrun with weeds and chimney pinks and day
lilies. Once-cherished flower gardens ran wild over the
years. The stagecoaches no longer whirled up to the taverns
with news of the outside world for the eager villagers who
lived by the back-country crossroads. Hearty stage drivers
no longer tooted their horns and called out messages at the
lonely farmhouses in the hills, or ran errands and made
purchases in town, or shepherded children on visits to relatives.

Deserted taverns, with windows staring blackly and
shutters banging, became the haunted houses of the villages.
The precious glass panes were broken, and bricks tumbled
into the fireplaces in the dusty, empty bedchambers.

 The city

Many other weary farmers stayed on in New England but
left the countryside and took paying jobs in the mills and
factories in the gray, unattractive cities. Whole families
went to work in the textile mills. Many of the operations
could easily be done by children, and little girls from six to
twelve years old were considered ideal for the work. They
picked over the cotton, spun on the spinning jenny, filled
quills with thread for the looms, and changed bobbins from
time to time.

The early factory owners tried to make conditions pleas-
ant enough for the children, and many older girls lived in
decent boardinghouses in cities like Lowell. They saved
their wages and sent money home to put their brothers
through college or pay off the mortgage on the hill farm
where they were born.

Still, children who had once run barefoot through the meadows were working indoors, twelve hours a day, six days a week. Very small children sometimes played unattended outside the mills while their mothers and sisters worked inside.

Quite a few farm boys hired out for pitifully low wages to tend the farms of the men who ran the factories.

Once the millworkers' families needed money to pay for their needs, they found they seldom had enough. Instead of raising everything they needed themselves (and being reasonably secure and comfortable), they quickly used up their cash wages to buy their food and clothing. They bought butter and cheese from the farmer neighbor, although they often kept a cow for milk and raised some beans and corn and chickens. Mothers made clothes for their children out of store-bought cotton cloth instead of homespun linen.

Many millworkers' children dropped out of school for good, and newcomers from foreign countries often did not attend school either, because they could not speak English. The states began to try much harder to establish up-to-date schools and train teachers. Many towns finally put up attractive schoolhouses with real desks sized according to the pupils' ages, and heated by pot-bellied stoves or even basement furnaces. State laws limited the number of hours children could work in the mills, but the limits were still very unfair.

Gradually, people and entire districts found it wise and profitable to specialize in one job or one product, and depend on the people of other regions to supply the rest of their wants and needs. New England's rivers and streams made it a natural center for manufacturing shoes, textiles, hardware, and furniture, and many New Englanders

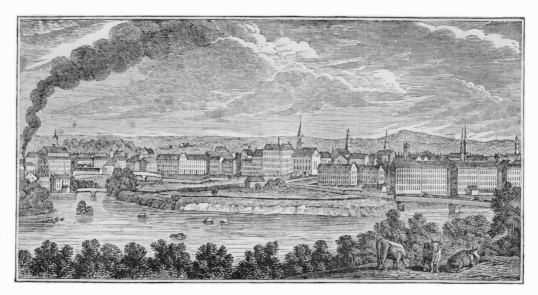

"East view of Lowell" by John Warner Barber.
Society for the Preservation of New England Antiquities.

seemed to have a natural talent for running a business or managing a mill.

Furniture shops and forges and shoemaking sheds and sawmills and pottery shops no longer served only their own villages and districts. They turned out extra nails or boxes or linseed oil to offer for sale elsewhere, and the roads and railroads made shipping no problem. And almost everything was sold for cash, not bartered.

 A different world

A hundred or a hundred and fifty years ago, every country man and wife, and even every farm boy and girl, knew quite a bit about ten or more trades and skills. It was really possible, and commonplace, for one man, one family, one village to get along in life very comfortably without depending on help "from outside"—at least as long as everyone worked hard, wasted nothing, and possessed a reasonable amount of common sense.

It was a simple way of life but a safe one, and there were plenty of chances to take personal pride in a job well done, from start to finish.

One enterprising New Hampshire cooper, in the 1830's, made cider barrels, butter tubs, cheese hoops, applesauce tubs, dippers, bowls, and assorted household woodenware. For several weeks each spring he peddled his own woodenware through the hills.

He *also* made and sold quill pens, mended boots and made shoes, wove bed ticking, peddled knitted goods as an agent for the local housewives, recorded village births, rented out his horse by the hour, boarded calves in the summertime, and pulled teeth (eight cents each, two for twelve)!

He certainly was clever, and yet he was probably not much busier than any other man of his village.

But the young American republic was growing up, and it was time for New England to cast its lot as a working partner in "Our Union," beside the middle states and the south and the wide, unexplored plains and mountains of the vast west.

For the first time, many New England boys and girls were not sure what they would be and where they would live when they grew up. For some, there was no more homestead to inherit, no fields and woodlots to tend, and no friendly, familiar neighbors to grow up with. The seasons of the year passed almost unnoticed in the crowded, gray mill towns.

The country folk who kept to their old ways found that life did become a little easier. There were cookstoves and matches, and sewing machines and paper patterns, indoor pumps and good new tools, and a wide variety of household goods in the stores. But they knew they would not be able to afford all the things they would have loved to own.

So, after the middle of the nineteenth century there was no turning back the hands of the old grandfather clock to the "age of homespun," when the jack-of-all-trades was king. The wide world just around the river bend and over the mountain had opened up, and more and more of the boys and girls of New England left the old farms behind to make their way in that wide and busy world.

The seasons come, the seasons go,
And God be good to all.

Suggested Further Reading

MOST of the books and other sources I have used in writing this book are old, out of print, and not available in general libraries. I read memoirs and "recollections" by nineteenth-century New Englanders, as well as many town and county histories, particularly of southern New Hampshire, the region I know best. There are, however, a number of publications generally available that would bring great pleasure to readers who have enjoyed this book. An informal list of them follows.

The publications of Old Sturbridge Village: the series of over twenty illustrated booklets, the quarterly *New-England Galaxy*, and the newsletter *The Rural Visitor*.

Noah Webster's *American Spelling Book*, available in a facsimile paperback edition published by Teachers College of Columbia University in the Classics in Education series.

Ordinary old schoolbooks, which can sometimes be found at surprisingly low prices in secondhand bookstores. They are best when they bear the marks of use, such as names, scribbles, notes, and even forgotten bookmarks.

Poems of John Greenleaf Whittier, especially "Snow-Bound: A Winter Idyl," "The Barefoot Boy," "The Old Burying-Ground," "To My Old Schoolmaster," "A Song of Harvest," "In School-Days," "April," "Telling the Bees," and "The Drovers" and "The Huskers" from "Songs of Labor."

"The Village Blacksmith" by Henry Wadsworth Longfellow and "The September Gale" by Oliver Wendell Holmes.

The current issue of *The Old Farmer's Almanac*. It has been published every year since 1792. Its format has not changed through the years, although the word "Old" was added in 1832 to distinguish it from imitators.

Biographies, autobiographies, and memoirs of well-known New Englanders of country background, such as Daniel Webster, Horace Greeley, P. T. Barnum, the Beecher family, Whittier, Ralph Waldo Emerson, Louisa May Alcott, Susan B. Anthony, and many more.

Rewarding books of fairly recent date, or reissue, are:

Earle, Alice Morse, *Child Life in Colonial Days*, New York, Macmillan, 1899; 16th printing, 1959.
———, *Home Life in Colonial Days*, New York, Macmillan, 1898; 20th printing, 1950. (Many American Colonial ways lasted well into the nineteenth century in rural areas.)
Hale, Edward Everett, *A New England Boyhood*, Boston, Little, Brown, reissued 1964. (The childhood of a wealthy Boston boy.)
Johnson, Clifton, *Old-time Schools and School-books*, New York, Macmillan, 1904. (Many pictures and entertaining anecdotes.)
Langdon, William Chauncy, *Everyday Things in American Life, 1776–1876*, Vol. II, New York, Scribner's, 1941.
Lipman, Jean, *American Folk Decoration*, New York, Oxford, 1951.
Mitchell, Edwin Valentine, *It's an Old New England Custom*, New York, Vanguard, 1946.
Mussey, Barrows, *Old New England*, New York, A. A. Wyn, 1946.
Rawson, Marion Nicholl, *New Hampshire Borns a Town*, New York, Dutton, 1942. (A long but very readable story of the birth and growth of a country village.)
Sandrof, Ivan, *Massachusetts Towns—An 1840 View*, Barre, Mass., Barre Publishers, 1963. (Wood engravings by John Warner Barber, who jogged over the roads of Massachusetts in the late 1830's in his one-horse wagon and sketched over three hundred towns.)
Sloane, Eric, *Folklore of American Weather*, New York, Duell, Sloan & Pearce, 1963.
Train, Arthur, Jr., *The Story of Everyday Things*, New York, Harper, 1941.
Tunis, Edwin, *Colonial Living*, New York and Cleveland, World, 1957. (Unusually clear illustrations and explanatory text.)

Index

accidents, 14–15, 99
accounts:
    farmers', 11–12, 38
    storekeepers', 24–25
American Spelling Book, 44
animals (*see also* cattle; oxen;
    sheep), 1–2, 19, 58, 63, 66–67,
    74, 81, 90, 107–108, 111–112,
    125–127
apples, 114–116
arithmetic, 45–46

"Babbatassett Village, Pepperell,
    Massachusetts, View of"
    (Smith), 134
"Baby in Red Chair" (unknown),
    31
"Baby in Wicker Basket" (Stock),
    88
baking, 48–49
baptism, 50
barter, 22, 137
baths, 87
beds, 7–8, 12, 118
Bible, the, 12, 42–44, 51, 89
birch brooms, 9
birds, 1–2, 58, 63, 66–67, 81, 90,
    107, 111, 122–123
blacksmiths, 6, 33–34, 63
blizzards, 16, 31–32, 134

"boarding round," 39–40
books (*see also* schoolbooks), 31,
    40, 50
borning room, 13
"Boys in a Pasture" (Homer), 80
"boys' pew," 51
bread, *see* baking; "rye-and-
    Injun"
bridges:
    covered, 33, 58
    toll, 62
"Brighton (central part), Western
    View of" (Barber), 124
burying grounds, 85–86, 115
butter, 25–26, 102

"Canada Settlers in Sugar Camp
    in Snowstorm" (Harvey), 56
candles, 8, 76
candy, 23
cattle, 102, 108
cattle shows, 124–125
cattle traders, 123–124
"change-work," 29
cheese, 102–103, 105
chores (*see also* fire; flax; haying;
    housework; washday), 8–9,
    59, 65, 102, 115, 126–127
    on the Sabbath, 87
    at school, 34, 36–37, 44–45

Christmas, 129–130
"Church at Westfield Farms, Massachusetts" (Durrie), 49
churches, *see* meetinghouses
cider, 115–116
"Cider Making" (Mount), 117
clothes, 7–8, 32–33, 82, 92–93, 121, 136
    militia uniforms, 73–74
    ministers', 49
    Sabbath and holiday, 87–88, 125
"cold years," 134
Concord River, 108
Connecticut River, 67
cooking (*see also* baking), 5, 16, 115–116
"Corn Husking" (Johnson), 119
corn husking bees, 117–118
"country pay," 23
"Country School, The" (Homer), 92–93
country stores, *see* stores, country
craftsmen:
    part-time, 6–7
    itinerant, 74–76

dancing, 29–30
dishes, *see* eating utensils
doctors, 13–14
drunkards, 61
dyes, 121

eating utensils, 4–6
Erie Canal, 134
Examination Day, 46–48

fairs, 125
Farmer's Almanac, The, 11, 118
"Farmers Nooning" (Mount), 106

fire, 2–4, 8, 32
    at school, 34
firewood, 18–20, 36
fishing, 1–2, 67–68, 113
flax, 100–102
flowers, 67, 81–84, 93, 96, 102, 111, 135
food, *see* baking; cooking; meals; snacks
footstoves, 49
Fourth of July, *see* Independence Day

game, 6, 122
games (*see also* sports), 82, 95, 118, 133
    at parties, 30
gingerbread, 63, 72
"Going to the Cider Mill" (Durrie), 122
grain, 109, 119–120
gravestones, 85
grist mills, *see* mills, grist

harvesting, 109, 112–115
haying, 105–106
herbs, 14, 113–114
"Hobby Horse, The" (unknown), 91
holidays, *see* cattle shows; Christmas; fairs; Independence Day; Muster Day; Sabbath; shearing; Thanksgiving; town meeting; wood hauling
"Home to Thanksgiving" (Currier and Ives), 130
"hooks and trammels," 42
"Horse in Full Gallop" (Davenport), 43
housework, 6, 9, 87

hunting, 122–123
hurricane, the great September, 87–88

illness, 13–15, 114
Independence Day, 96–98
Indians, 51, 56–57, 63, 96
Indian summer, 125–126
"Inn Scene—Winter" (Durrie), 21
insects, 50, 68, 81, 84, 107, 116
"Interior of the Moses Morse Farmhouse, Loudon, New Hampshire" (Leavitt), 75
ironware, 6–7

keeping room, 4, 31–32
kitchen, 4, 12
knitting, 7, 71
"Knitting for the Soldiers" (Johnson), 70

"Latest News, The, Cattle in Stable" (Tait), 69
"Long Island Farmhouses" (Mount), 110
Lowell, Massachusetts, 135–136
"Lowell, East view of" (Barber), 137

mail, 23
manufacturing (*see also* sawmills), 6–7, 135–137
maple sugar, *see* sugar, maple
market, trips to, 21–22
meals, 4–6, 20, 46, 48–50, 118
meat, preservation of, 127–128
medicines, 14, 16, 113–114
meetinghouses, 49–51
  falling asleep in, 89–90

"Melting Story, A," 25–26
merit certificates, 29, 47
Merrimack River, 108
militia, 71–74
"Militia Training" (Clonney), 73
millponds, 33, 65–66, 102
mills (*see also* sawmills):
  fulling, 121
  grist, 65, 112–113, 120
  textile, 10, 135–136
ministers, 30, 38, 46, 97
  clothing of, 49
  salary of, 20, 61
Monadnock, Grand, 123
money, 11, 46, 71
mud time, 58–59
Muster Day, 71–74

Nantucket Island, 68–69
Negroes, 51, 96
"New England Farm Landscape" (Durrie), 113
"New England Homestead" (Gerry), 86
"New England Interior, A" (Bosworth), 14
New England Primer, 43
"New England School" (Bosworth), 35
newspapers, 11, 23, 38, 76
nutmeg, 79
nuts, 32, 112

"Old Grist Mill, The" (Durrie), 54
oxen, 17–18, 63–64, 105

painters, 75–76
Patch, Jonas, 44–45
peddlers, 72, 77–79

penmanship, 42–43, 47
"Phillips Academy at Andover, Western View of" (Barber), 37
pigeon hunts, 123
Pike's *Arithmetic*, 46
planting, 63–65, 100
poor, care of the, 60–62
pottery, 4, 114
prayers, family, 12, 51, 90
"Princeton, View of the central part of" (Barber), 59
Puritans, 129

quilting, 29
"Quilting Party, The" (unknown), 28

railroads, 134, 137
raisings, 98–100
"Raymond, Joseph and Anna" (unknown), 132
"Returning to the Farm" (Durrie), 19
"Reverend John Atwood and His Family, The" (Darby), 52–53
Revolution, 72, 96
roads:
    breaking out, 16–18
    construction of, 62–63
    in mud time, 58–59
"rye-and-Injun," 48, 120

Sabbath, 27, 48–51, 86–90, 130
samplers, 28, 94
sawmills, 16, 18, 65
schoolbooks, 42–46
schoolhouses, 34–37
schoolmasters, 38–41
    salary of, 60–61

schoolmistresses, 38, 93
"Schoolroom: Teacher Striking Boy's Hand" (unknown), 39
schools:
    district (*see also* schoolbooks; schoolhouses; schoolmasters; schoolmistresses), 34–48, 91–96
    town, 136
"Scythe Grinder, The" (Edmonds), 104
sewing (*see also* quilting), 7–8, 76, 91
shearing, 68–70
sheep (*see also* shearing), 33–34, 120
"sheep's-gray," 121
shoes, 33, 59, 89
shows, traveling, 74
singing school, 30–31
slaughtering, 68, 127–128
sleighbells, 20
"Sleigh Ride, The" (Clonney), 32
sleighrides, 28
slips, 50–51
"Smith, Jesse Kittredge, Dr." (Woolson), 15
snacks, 20, 63, 67, 72, 84, 96, 112, 114–115, 118
"Snap the Whip" (Homer), 95
soap, 128
spelling, 44–45
    bees, 30, 47
spinning:
    of flax, 101–102
    of wool, 70–71
sports (*see also* games), 33–34, 82, 100
stagecoaches, 135
stores, country, 22–26

sugar:
    maple, 55–58
    white, 56, 121
"Summer Farm Scene" (Durrie),
    64
"Summer Landscape" (Durrie),
    103
Sunday, see Sabbath
supper parties, 28–29, 51

tailors, 76
taverns, 18, 22, 135
taxes, 36, 60
tea parties, 101–102
teeth, care of, 13
"Temple, New Hampshire, View
    of" (Smith), 60–61
Thanksgiving, 129–133
"Tilton Family, The" (Davis), 10
tinware, decorated, 78–79
tolls, 62–63
town meeting, 59–63, 99
toys, 9–10, 78–79, 82, 84, 87, 131
Training Day, see Muster Day
treen, 5
trees, 19–20, 56, 58, 67, 111–112,
    115
"Truant Gamblers, The"
    (Mount), 83
trunnels, 98
turnpikes, 62–63

"Two Children with Dog Minny
    on a Pink Ribbon" (Prior),
    27

valentine, 30
"Village Post Office" (Wood), 24
villages, population of, 96

wanderers, 111
washday, 128
"Washington, General, on Horse"
    (Willson), 97
weather, clues to, 108, 127
weaving, 76, 120–121
Webster, Noah, 44
weddings, 29
wells, 94
West, the, 134
"West Rock" (Durrie), 107
whittling, 9–10, 84, 98
"Winter Farm Scene" (Durrie),
    xii
woodenware (see also whittling), 6
wood hauling, 18–20
"Woodshed Interior" (unknown),
    99
Wordwell, Memorus, 44–45

"Yankee Peddler," (Ehninger), 78
"Younger Generation, The"
    (Prior), 3

ABOUT THE AUTHOR

The traditions of country life that she describes in HUCKLEBERRY HILL are very familiar to Elizabeth Gemming. She is a descendant of the earliest settlers of New England, and has spent part of every summer at the family homestead in southern New Hampshire.

Mrs. Gemming was graduated from Wellesley College and has studied and taught in Germany on a Fulbright scholarship. She has worked as an editor and translator, and with her husband, the distinguished book designer Klaus Gemming, has written several books for children. The Gemmings and their two young daughters now live in New Haven, Connecticut.